# Part One

Eighteen and full of hope

## So it Begins

In the beginning there were two.

Myself, eighteen years old, wide eyed, naïve and full of wonder. My childlike excitement ever present but mostly hidden. No self esteem, yet bizarrely far too trusting. I had been hurt, dejected, was desperately seeking acceptance, love, a place in the world.

There was also HE. Older, hardened, seemingly wiser, a serious nature that offered a perceived protection. His silliness only apparent whilst under the influence of the readily available weed source.

At a time when "home" was non existent, when family had disintegrated, HE seemed an answer. Maybe in HIM I could find the stability I craved.

It was a fresh new Millennium, early summer 2001 in the idyllic setting of the Costa del Sol. Adventures could be found around ever corner. The sun shone brightly, as did the glowing tips of the endless joints. It was an illusion of perfection.

HE and I had only been a couple since May, we shared a group of friends. Over that three months the others seemed to drift away, more and more it was just the two of us.

I was introduced to an older couple, HE said they had helped him to move over, that HE looked upon them as surrogate parents. I think I fell more in love with them and their carefree lifestyle than I ever fell for HIM.

She was an artist, in her fifties with two grown children, full of fascinating stories and ideologies. Her partner, though a decade younger was a laugh a minute and utterly devoted to her. The pair of them were so affectionate and loving, their home filled with music, raucous laughter and constant dancing. They sold it. They sold HIM. Happy times were many. More so whilst in their company.

When it was just the two of us he was surly. I felt childish and judged. I would be chastised for being myself, for having flights of fancy or expressing a feeling HE didn't agree with. I brushed it off, swallowed the lump in my throat, put it down to the fact that HE was older, HE knew things, I was after all just a stupid kid.

August rolled in yet apparently my monthly gift from mother nature did not. HE told me I was late and needed to take a test. So we took a walk to the local Farmacia.

Well, there it was. Eighteen years old, three months into the first adult relationship I had experienced, knocked up!

Thrilled and terrified in equal measure, thoughts were racing through my young mind.

I was living abroad, I had no insurance, I wasn't working, how could I afford to provide for a baby.

HE seemed pleased, in a matter of fact kind of way. HE phoned his family over in the UK to let them know the news. I arranged for us to visit my mother's that evening. There was no discussion, no options, no realities. Apparently we were having a baby, together and that was that.

At that time HE would travel back to the UK once per month or so to carry out work as a merchandiser. At least, that's what HE told me.

When you're young and resident in a place where everyone you know is running or hiding from something you quickly learn not to ask questions. So the day that I was searching in the kitchen for a chopping board and came across a huge wedge of cash, I had simply put it back where I found it mentioning nothing of it.

Perhaps HE hadn't opened a Spanish bank account, it was none of my business anyway. But, maybe HE could financially support this baby.

Years later it transpired that HE was in fact a drug runner, the money had been from a run. The trips to do merchandising were drug runs.

A few weeks passed by, morning noon and night sickness had arrived. That pregnancy glow people speak of, was simply a nauseated sheen of sweat.

We had spent a pleasant evening with the older couple before returning to HIS bedsit. Music was softly playing as we wound down for sleep. HE had been withdrawn, short and snappy for most of the day. I thought maybe HE was tired but unfortunately it was more than that. HE told me that his son, who had been seven at the time, was acting up, was asking for his Daddy. Poor lad, I thought, he must really miss HIM.

So the ultimatum was laid before me.

HE was moving back to the UK as soon as possible to be there for his son. I could either move back with HIM, bring our child up together as a family; or I stay in Spain, never to hear from HIM again. It was very clear, if I chose to stay, I was on my own.

So I did what any terrified, pregnant teenager would do. I chose family. I chose to move back with HIM, back to the UK, to be part of HIS life so that HE would be a part of both HIS children's.

# Bitter cold

HE came from a very different background to me.

I hailed from a small town in Bedfordshire, famed for it's airport, HE, from the cold North East.

The picture HE had painted of where we were to live was bleak. Akin to Belfast, is how HE had described it. Riots in the streets, kidnappings, random attacks for a sideways glance. A place in which HE and his brother's were notorious, where people crossed the street in fear of them. To say I had feelings of apprehension would be widely understated.

I had never felt so vulnerable. Sure I had been in a few dangerous situations before but when there is a tiny life growing inside of you, the realisation of your own fragility is intense.

I viewed it all as an adventure. Part of the narrative in a gritty British film.

We moved into his mother's. The two of us in a single bed surrounded by the toys of his four year old niece.

HIS mother was a loud, brash, chain-smoking, hard drinking northern woman. The house reeked of smoke, years old that permeated the walls mixed with plumes of freshly exhaled tobacco smoke with heady undertones of stale chip fat. This did absolute wonders for my 24 hour a day sickness.

The first week or so I vomited that much that the acrid taste of bile was a normality. HE would awaken early and go out, leaving me alone with HIS family. I tried to venture out into the living room a few times, the smells made me heave plus the constant stream of noisy inquisitive visitors was too much, I felt like a shiny new toy being paraded around to all who heard of me. So I vomited and stayed sequestered in the bedroom, for which I was shouted at.

It was rude, the sickness wasn't that bad, I was being pathetic.

I had made a mistake. I wept for the life I had left behind. I wept at my stupidity.

I was stuck with no money, in a place so unfamiliar, nowhere to run and nobody to turn to.

I dried my tears, tried my best to swallow my feelings and got on with it.

After a month or two of staying at his mother's and in one of his friends back rooms, we rented a place of our own. A flat above a shop, opposite the courts.

It was grotty but had high ceilings and was a space for just us. I could listen to my own music again, read my books undisturbed. I borrowed baby books from the library, imagined how my beautiful little one was progressing.

Come November the cold was biting. I had never shivered so much. We would walk pretty much everywhere. My hands forever numb. I desperately missed the mild Spanish winter, longed to feel the gentle warmth of the sun on my skin.

I'd had this idea of motherhood, of the type of Mumma I would be.

The image I held was of a barefoot Mumma in a flowing summer dress, babe on hip and toddler at my feet, sun beaming down as I hung the washing and played with my darling little miracles. I would home school them, so they could be independent thinkers rather than becoming moulded robots. We would play music together, laughter would ring out constantly. A care free existence filled with love. This idea was slowly being dragged away. Apparently my long held desire to be a stay at home Mumma meant that I was lazy and entitled. I dared to point put that as HE wasn't working yet was physically able, perhaps it wasn't myself that was the lazy one. This seemed to spur HIM into action, a few days later he left for a weeks work away merchandising.

HE had left before I awoke. I got myself up and pottered into the living room where HE had left a note. At the bottom a P.S

"I've been meaning to ask you this for a while but can't seem to say it.

Will you marry me?"

I text HIM my answer.

A few hours later HE came home. The vehicle they had been travelling in had broken down, the job cancelled. So the next day we went to the registry office and booked our no frills wedding for two weeks time.

My Mum and sister's flew over from Spain, My Dad flew up from down south.

There were no flowers, no pomp, it poured with rain and I wore a black top and trousers as I signed the form agreeing to live beside this man forever. My baby would be born to married parents, would be so loved. Roll on May.

## Then there were three

As my bump grew, so too did my excitement. A name had been chosen, a male and a female, but I was certain she was a girl.

At the gender scan baby had been bouncing around like a little monkey, so it was purely a guessing game. But I knew. My little baby girl was growing stronger in spite of my daily vomiting.

I was under a close eye by the midwives. They suspected I was being abused and were certain I was depressed. I tried to assure them that it was merely circumstantial, that I was just homesick, that once I held my baby, everything would be fine. They didn't believe me.

I'm not sure that I believed myself.

I was now being taken to appointments by HIS older cousin. HE had been banned from the surgery for shouting at the Dr and dragging me out by my wrist as I furiously apologised to her. The birth grew nearer and the checks more frequent.

I had unexplained pains so spent a few days in day assessment hooked up to monitors. They discovered that my growing dumpling was double breech. This meant that if she hadn't moved in time she would be exiting my body bottom first. That would have been dangerous for the both of us. They could manually turn her, which carried a risk of miscarriage, or they could book me in for a caesarean section.

I opted for the Caesarean if she hadn't turned by herself. I begged her not to turn, I was so unprepared and scared of giving birth. Nobody had answered my questions on what to expect. I hadn't been allowed to attend any classes, HE knew everything from when HIS exes had had babies. So I had no idea how I would know when baby was coming or how much pain there would be.

Time continued to tick by, she continued to sit bum first. So they booked me in and I breathed a sigh of relief.

A week before she was due to arrive we moved into a flat a few miles away. Smaller but much nicer.

I went through all the baby bits, made sure there was nothing missing. We were ready.

Mum arrived from Spain the night before. She was accompanying me into theatre as HE had refused.

At two fifteen pm on Wednesday the eighth of May 2002, I felt a strange tugging sensation as my beautiful baby was plucked from my womb.

Mum whispered to me that she was a girl and tears sprang from my eyes. They checked her over before placing her next to my head. My perfect tiny bubba. I was a Mumma

This tiny person was the most important person ever to be created, it was now my job to give her the best life, the happiest life. She deserved my undivided attention. I was completely in love and ready to be the best Mumma I could be.


When she was three days old we could take her home. I was breastfeeding and enjoying every second of bonding with her.

Everyone that met her fell in love. How could they not. HE was playing proud Daddy and showing her off at every opportunity.

At two weeks she grew a little unsettled. She was hungry and unfortunately my itty bitty titties just weren't making enough for her. So I bit the bullet and gave her some formula. Happy baby once more.

A day after I moved her over to formula I had asked HIM to do one of the night feeds. HE refused. So I got up and fed her, I didn't mind, I was just a bit tired, thought we could share the load. 6 a.m. feed came around, I got up quietly and fed her, she was just about finished when HE got up.

Why hadn't I woken HIM, HE had said that HE was doing the morning. I apologised, told HIM I was awake anyway and didn't mind. Then all hell broke loose.

HE had shouted before, but I'd thought once we were both parents and a little person was around it would change.

Everything I was doing was wrong. I wasn't the person HE thought I was. I asked HIM to stop as I didn't want the baby upset. How dare I tell HIM what to do, who did I think I was. I was ordered to get her ready as he was going out.

I prepared a few bottles, packed her nappy bag, made sure she was clean and comfortable.

HE screamed some more then told me I had a decision to make, I had to decide where I wanted a ticket to. I was either going to Spain or Luton and he was keeping the baby. The fear I felt from that threat. The bottom just fell out of my world. HE can't have my baby.

HE left, I rang my Mum sobbing. She asked if I thought that's why HE had married me, so HE had parental rights.

It had transpired that the son HE moved back for had actually been adopted at eighteen months old. That whole, "My son needs me" tale had been nothing more than a story. So now my head was spinning, I'd been used.

HE had what it was HE wanted. HE was going to take away my sunshine. My reason for living. I had no idea what to do. HE was always spouting out about rights. HE knew HIS. I had no clue.

Fortunately it blew over, he apologised, we moved on.

We visited Spain, everyone there fell in love with her.

We then decided to move to Luton. So the three of us moved into my Dad's and life looked a little brighter.

# Blissful Domesticity

HE actually got a job in Luton. So life started to resemble something akin to normal.

I took care of my angel, I cleaned, I did the laundry, I even cooked.

I was enjoying being useful. My Dad had a physically demanding job, I liked the idea that he could come home to a hot meal and a clean house. I was content in taking care of my baby, my husband and my Dad. I would take baby to my Nan's, we were close, I had lived with her before we moved to Spain, it was wonderful to spend time with her and watch her bonding with her great granddaughter.

My Grandad's house was within walking distance of our house, so I would regularly take a stroll round to visit him, his wife and my aunt.

I was happy. Baby was happy. But HE wasn't.

A row erupted when Dad was out. I don't remember the catalyst, it really didn't take much, more often than not it was a perceived slight anyway. So screaming commenced. HE was going back to the North east. Fine, go, I didn't really care. Then it came, I was to pack a bag for the baby as HE was taking her with HIM. HE stormed upstairs to get a bag, I grabbed a blanket and the baby and bolted barefoot out of the door. I left it open so that he wouldn't be alerted to the sound and I ran.

I held my angel and sprinted as fast as I safely could away from HIM and the threat HE posed. I turned off the main street and headed into a cul-de-sac, I saw a house with lights ablaze and obvious signs of life and I banged on the door.

A lovely family let me in. They tried to calm me down, obviously concerned. I explained briefly, asked them to call a taxi. I sat on their stairs waiting for the taxi, whilst the ladies cooed over baby's big blue eyes.

As the Taxi pulled onto the main road I could see HIM walking up, shouting my name, I ducked down so he couldn't see, the taxi drove on to my Nan's house.

Nanny paid the driver, I told her why I'd fled. She was convinced that HE had hit me as I was so clearly terrified. I explained I was just scared of HIM taking baby.

My Dad came round a few hours later, he'd arrived home from the gym to find HIM crying, not knowing where we were. Dad knew exactly where we would be and had come to get us.

I didn't want to go back, but HE was my husband, I needed to hear HIM out. So off we went back to Dad's house, this incident, as was the last, brushed under the carpet.


The year progressed, Christmas was approaching. Baby's first Christmas. I had bought her a beautiful red tartan dress for the day. Baby and I were going to spend the day at Dad's girlfriend's. She had two children around 10 and 11, so it was to be a happy family day. HE didn't do Christmas. So it was just Dad, baby, myself and Dad's girlfriend's family. It was a truly lovely day. We were both spoilt, the food was delicious, the company great. Just as Christmas should be.


Quite soon into the new year, HE decided we were moving. HE was working two jobs but wasn't happy, HE wanted to leave. HE said we should go somewhere that we knew someone, so the choices were Dorset or Huddersfield.

Reluctantly I helped pack the car and we left for Huddersfield, tears streaming down my face as I watched my own happiness fade into the distance.

We went to the council and HE spun a tale that we were being pursued by people that wanted to harm us. We were placed in a bed and breakfast above a pub in Dewsbury whilst sufficient accommodation could be found.

It was a single room with a single bed a sink and a small tv. Baby had her travel cot beside the bed. It was dark, dank and noisy. The other residents scared me. I still didn't understand why we had to leave Luton. HE spent the evenings in the pub downstairs whilst I sat in the room with baby. Some nights HE went further afield drinking in the town after the pub was closed.

After a week or so we were allocated a house. A two up, two down on a corner plot. There was a play park a few doors down. I could make this home.

The day we were due to move in, HE had a change of heart. The car was packed, HE handed them back the keys, told them no thank you. HE told me that HE had realised there was a drug dealer living on the street behind, that HE needed back up should trouble find it's way to the door. So back to the North east we did go.

Back to his mothers. A different residence but same set up. A single bed in his niece's room. We didn't stay long. An argument kicked off and his older brother threatened me, I wanted to leave, not that I had wanted to be there in the first instance.


This time, we headed to Spain.

We stayed with the older couple in their beach side caravan. It was lovely to be with them and the colourful visitors that came by each day. Life was beginning to look up again.

They were helping us to find an apartment, had set HIM up with a job at Gibraltar hospital as a cleaner.

We moved into the apartment on the border town beside Gibraltar, the couple had given us a puppy. Baby and puppy were bonding. I could make this home.

The day before HE was due to start work, we got the bus to visit my Mother. It was an hour or so journey, but felt so good to be able to just hop on a bus and visit.

We enjoyed the time it was a lovely day . Then HE pulled me aside, told me to ask if we could stay. I was instantly confused. People had gone out of their way to help us, set us up in a nice apartment, gifted us a pet and gone to the trouble of finding HIM employment. But HE didn't want to live in La Linea.

So I asked and Mum agreed it was ok, HE travelled back the next day to get our belongings. It was nice spending time with Mum, so I focused on that.

A few weeks later I discovered that baby was going to be a big sister. They would be eighteen months apart, perfect, I thought. They would always have a friend. I was so excited.

But, once again here I was, abroad, no job, HE wasn't working, no insurance. So, I found a job. I thought to myself that if he wouldn't fulfil his role and provide for us, maybe I could. So I found a job. I wasn't particularly au fait with the line of work, but we needed the money. I hated being away from baby, but I kept reminding myself that I was doing it for her and the gorgeous new addition in progress.

A few weeks into working life, HE interviewed for the same job and was successful. We took it in turns for a while, alternating morning and afternoon shifts.

I started to suffer morning sickness and judging on my last pregnancy HE convinced me to quit and stay home with bubba. HE was now solely responsible for our financial wellbeing,

Baby's first birthday arrived, she loved her few gifts and was settling into her personality more by the day. She and I spent wonderful days in the sunshine. That image I held of motherhood was eking it's way into a possibility. Happy sun kissed babies.

Then HE was fired.

HE flew back to the UK to try and sort something with money.

Whilst HE was away I came to the realisation that there was no option for progression if we stayed in Spain. HE expressed a desire to train as a plumber, so back to Luton we did move.

I was relieved in a way. I was by now around four and a half months pregnant and hadn't yet seen a Dr.

We moved back in with my Dad.

HE didn't stay long, HE went back up to the north east. I can't remember the reasoning. But I didn't really care. It was easier to cope day to day without risk of upsetting him. I was happily back with my Dad and visiting with my Nan regularly. Besides baby kept me pretty busy, I just settled into a routine with her. I loved being a Mumma.

Dad moved house whilst we were with him.

Baby number two was growing steadily as was the bump that housed them. The Summer was hot, I was uncomfortable, but content with our lot.

Along came September and news that HE had found a house for us to move into. So off we went again. A new home, a new area, new family members to get to know.

# Family of Four

There had been so much upheaval and displacement in that past year and a half, at all times baby plus growing bubs were my priority. As long as they were ok, I could be happy. It felt nice to be able to sit back in a home that was just ours and try to be that family unit HE had promised. I had loved being near my Dad and Nan, but to just worry about baby, to focus completely on her needs, it felt right.

She was doing so well. Hitting all her milestones, she could recognise shapes, knew her colours. She could even show me simple words in her favourite books. She was such a happy girlie, she was also excited to be a big sister. I would point out other babies when we were out and about, explain that soon we would have one at home. She would rock her dolls and kiss them. In spite of all the moves, all the adjusting to new places, new people, sometimes Dadda, sometimes not; she had always had me, her only constant through it all.

I was glad that was all she seemed to need and was thriving. She made being a Mumma so easy. Best job in the world.

We settled into our new routine, the closer my due date got, the worse I felt. Not because of the new baby, I could not wait to meet the little bundle. All the necessary bits and pieces were ready. Baby and I would sing to the bump, she would stroke it and talk to it. That part was pure bliss.

It was HIM.

We were shouted at, a lot. HE wasn't a good Daddy. HE would full on shout at her for the silliest of reasons, when really, at that age, shouting isn't really necessary.

If I hadn't done something HE thought that I should have done, I was screamed at.

I was lazy, useless. If I cried, I was pathetic.

I began to treasure the times HE was out. When baby and I were at peace.

I feared what adding the new baby would be like. Maybe HE was just stressed and once Bubs arrived HE would mellow. I would watch happy families as they went about their lives, I longed for that. I wasn't loved here.

I tried sitting down with HIM. I told HIM that I was scared of HIM, that the environment wasn't a healthy or happy place to be in, for myself or baby. HE apologised, promised to be more aware. Blamed it on the stress of looking for work.

Things grew calmer, for a while.


The week of my due date was upon us. Baby and I went down for breakfast. HE had already left. HE would always wake early and leave the house. One of HIS cousin's had moved around the corner with her husband. HE would spend most days there, getting high.

I had given up smoking weed when baby had arrived. It affected my ability to be fully present as a Mumma. Being a Mumma was a high enough for me. Nothing will ever beat the rush when the perfect being you created smiles up at you. I loved every second.

Baby was eating raisins and building a tower out of coloured blocks when there was a knock at the door.

I went to answer it, it was the postman. I couldn't open the door. We were locked in. The postman had to pass the parcel through a window. Then it dawned on me.

I was nine months pregnant, could go into labour at any given second, yet every morning when HE left, HE was locking us both in the house. What if I went into Labour?

I rang HIM, asked HIM to come home. HE told me HE was on a message, would be back soon. Four hours passed before HE returned.

From the next morning the key was posted through the letterbox so that if I needed to escape, I could.

The week ended, heartburn remained, new baby seemed rather too comfy. Labour stayed away.

So the windows were thoroughly scrubbed, big baby and I practiced some serious moshing around the living room. Lots of fun was had in an attempt to budge new baby.

Eight days past my due date around 9pm, tightness had been escalating since before big baby's bedtime routine, which lasted from 6 until 7.

I told HIM the pains were getting stronger, that we should think about heading to the hospital soon. HE took that as the perfect time for HIM to go for a nap and went to bed. Said HE was going to try and get a couple of hours in, to wake HIM when contractions were five minutes apart.

Forty five minutes later they were around seven, maybe six minutes apart. I began to panic. HE had said five, but this was my first labour, I was scared, I wanted to go the hospital. I was afraid to wake HIM, it hadn't been long, HE hated to be woken unnecessarily. The pain grew more intense. It was now an hour after HE had gone to bed. I woke him with trepidation. HE got up, his cousin came over to watch big baby, I grabbed my bag and we set off.

We got so far along on our journey when HE announced we needed to stop for fuel.

I grit my teeth, pushed my foot on the dash board, this hurt like nothing I had ever felt before. I now understood what all those women meant when they would simply answer that when in labour, I would know. It felt like forever before we were moving again.

Once at the hospital everything ran smoothly.

I tried Gas and air for the pain, but it made me vomit.

They tried me with Pethidine, but that slowed everything down.

So I requested an epidural, suddenly it all became easy.

My body did as it was supposed to do and eventually out she came.

A raven haired angel, pink and squawky. Baby girl had entered the world.

She had so much hair she was like a baby Elvis. She had dark eyes to match her dark hair, so different to her big sister. HE went home and I was left with my new beautiful daughter.

I was a bit concerned, the rush of feelings that I had felt the first time were absent. It felt different. She was perfect. I fed her, spoke to her, promised her that she would be loved. We stayed in hospital for two days, we had no visitors.

HE came to collect us in the car of another of his cousin's girlfriend, whom I had never met before. Our car had broken down. We went home to begin life as a family of four.

Big Girl walked straight up to the Moses basket baby girl was laid in, she pointed, "Bubba"? she asked, then gently kissed her forehead.

I sat Big Girl on the sofa and softly laid Baby Girl on her lap. She carefully stroked her hair, beaming down with love. The bond was set. My girls.


It was the next day that the fierce rush of love struck me.

HE had a friend out front, fixing the car. Big girl was having a nap, Baby Girl had just been fed, happily cooing in her basket. HE deposited his friend's three year old in the living room, told me to watch her. I left her watching cartoons whilst I went to make HIM and his friend a cuppa. I had poured one mug, I heard little footsteps next to the door. There were two quite steep steps down into the kitchen, the floor cheap lino covered concrete.

In the doorway stood the three year old carrying Baby Girl by the scruff of her clothes. "Baby wants you".

There it was, Mumma instinct, full force! I calmly but quickly moved to pick up Baby Girl. I told the three year old thank you, said it was nice of her to want to help, but that next time she should just let the Mumma know if a baby needed them, not to pick them up. Not sure she understood, but I didn't want to startle her.

From then on, Mumma love was strong. I felt everything I was supposed to.

## Baby Blues

Big girl settled into life as a big sister very quickly. She loved her baby sister, she would stroke her face gently, sing her songs and draw her pictures. She was such a good girl. I made sure to tell her that regularly, I didn't want her to feel pushed aside. Her behaviour suggested she didn't. I had two arms and two hips, plus plenty of love and endless hugs for my two gorgeous girlies.

Baby girl was another hungry munchkin, so after two weeks I started her on formula. It was nice to be able to get Big girl involved, passing Mumma the bottle or helping me to place them in the steriliser. It was more to make her feel involved and appreciated than it was a real lean for help.

We settled into a nice routine, I would bathe both girls before stories and bed.

Of course at that stage Baby girl would be waking throughout the night for feeds and nappy changes, I just felt it was important to establish the routine early on. For both girls stability.

The Depression seemed to hit all of a sudden. I was waking around three times through the night to tend to Baby girl as a result I would sleep later than HIM come the morning.

This didn't last long as I was soon awoken by stomping and ranting, then a screaming angry man in my face.

I had left a teaspoon on the counter top!

I was such a lazy waste of space!

Fear set in again. I'd frantically make the extra effort each day to make sure nothing was out of place, but each morning I would lay in wait, panicking that I'd missed something, expecting the eruption.

Five days out of seven there would be something. I tiptoed around HIM.

One day he declared that we were buying a new sofa, HE had the cash from HIS last crop, we were off to pick one. I dressed both girls, packed the nappy bag, we headed out.

A nice normal family trip. Although it felt like we were playing at it, it still felt nice to be doing something together, as a normal family unit. Happy Babies, Happy Mumma.

Big girl and I followed HIM, HE carried Baby girl in a baby carrier. We went into several shops where upon the staff would fawn over the girls, HE would barter with them, insist on a deal because HE was paying cash.

It was fine to start with, but as the day drew on HIS patience dwindled, HIS attitude became aggressive, I was embarrassed to be stood with HIM. HE would shout at me in full earshot of anyone nearby. Calling me names, belittling me. I swallowed the tears and took the girls to the car as Baby girl needed a bottle. HE didn't like that, I was lambasted when HE returned to the car. How dare I disrespect him in public that way.

I tried to explain that I had needed to feed Baby girl, HE didn't care. We drove off. HE was still shouting. On the way home we stopped at some traffic lights, a student was taking too long to cross, so HE beeped, the student flipped HIM off and HE shot out of the car in a nano second. HE chased the poor kid down a side street, whilst I was stuck in traffic, in a car I couldn't drive, other cars beeping angrily, people staring as I tried to remain calm for the three month old baby and young toddler, tears were streaming down my face. I didn't know if HE was coming back. After what felt like an eternity HE returned, red faced and out of breath. Nothing was spoken, HE calmly drove us home.

I started to tell the health visitor that I wasn't happy. She had noticed already, had told me that the way HE spoke to me wasn't right. I made excuses, as a good wife should.

She advised me to see the Doctor, who subsequently put me on anti-depressants but also urged me to get away for a few days, to go visit family. I told the DR that I couldn't as I had no money. This apparently was a form of abuse. In controlling the money, HE was controlling me. Again, I made excuses.

Life continued, Big girl was talking more, could now speak in full sentences. Strangers were so impressed when they learnt her age. She was my little superstar.

Baby girl was beautiful, she started suffering with cholic, so special bottles and gripe water were purchased, days were spent bouncing her around the house singing, it seemed the only way to calm her.

Eventually the day came that the sofa was to be delivered. HE was out, so I showed the men where it was to go before unwrapping and testing it out.

I left Big girl downstairs playing whilst I nipped upstairs to put away some washing. She was waiting at the foot of the stairs eager to show me something. She had drawn me a beautiful picture, in biro, on the new sofa.

My heart fell through the floor, I was terrified. Why had I left a pen laying around, HE was going to kill me, or her, or both.

I calmly told Big girl that although it was a lovely drawing, she should not have drawn it on the sofa and it was naughty to have done so.

HE came home, took one look and flew into a rage.

HE picked her up from the floor and threw her onto the sofa before screaming at her.

HE smacked her hand, screamed some more. I tried to intervene, was shouted down, she needed disciplined.

HE continued screaming at her, told her she was grounded.

I carried my sobbing two year old to bed.

The screaming persisted behind me as I walked upstairs. My fault for having a pen, for leaving her long enough, what had I been doing?

Can't even keep watch over my own children, pathetic, useless.

I managed to get the pen out eventually. I now realised however just how little regard HE had for children's feelings. I understood she had done wrong, but the level of the shouting directed towards a two year old was insane.

I crept on eggshells around HIM. Making sure the babies weren't too loud if HE was home, that mess was contained away from HIS area.

# Mumma's instinct

I was referred to a group by the Health visitor. Mum's would sit, chat and craft in one room, whilst babies were taken care of in another room by nursery nurses. It was once a week. It was nice to meet with and speak to other Mum's, to share stories and advice.

Obviously I kept the worst parts of my home life private. I had been shoved around a fair bit. HE hadn't hit me, but if I became upset, or answered back during a telling off, I was shoved. HE choked me to the point of passing out in front of the babies. But that was my fault, for speaking out of turn.

On one occasion I had had enough, was giving back, telling HIM how HE was failing, HE pinned me to the floor, slapping me across the face with the back of HIS hand. I was hysterical apparently, needed to calm down.

I attended a group session with a black eye. Everyone wanted to know what had happened, I downplayed it. He'd been nice since, it had been my fault anyway. Least said, soonest mended. I brushed it under the carpet.

By this point HE had started working. It was after I had got myself a job in a brand new Debenhams. HE wouldn't let me do it. Said the travel costs were too high. It was five minutes on the bus, I'd cost it all up, it still worked out to be financially worth it. But I had to decline the offer. That had been a blow, I was really looking forward to a little independence. So anyway, HE got HIMSELF a job as a night security on a building site.

It meant I had to try extra hard to keep the Babies quiet during the day whilst HE slept. But we hardly saw HIM which was good.

I began taking driving lessons. An hour each time. I would pick an hour that HE would be awake before HE started work so that the Girls could stay home.

On one particular day HE told me to ask HIS cousin to watch them as HE wanted more sleep. So I arranged for the girls to be collected by HIS cousin and I would collect them once my lesson was over.

I let myself in the back door, HIS cousin was in the kitchen making cups of tea. My girl's were nowhere to be seen. I asked where they were and walked to where Baby girl was, Big girl was playing upstairs with the cousin's children I think.

Baby girl came toddling to me, she was ten months old at this point, I scooped her up and she clung to me. Bit odd I thought.

I had a cup of tea, then walked home so as not to disturb the girl's bedtime routine.

I gave them their evening meal, bathed them and put them to bed.

Baby girl was being more clingy than usual. She had always been quite an independent baby, not so fussed on hugs. But since picking her up she didn't seem to want me to put her down. My Mumma senses were tingling.

I wasn't sure if I was just being paranoid though as I always hated leaving them with others. The next day I was meant to be travelling to visit another of HIS cousin's girlfriends. I decided to carry on with the plan, I would ask her opinion. She had two older children.

She noticed the difference in Baby girl straight away. She backed up my fears and so the next morning I took the girl's along to the clinic, from there we were taken straight to a specialist unit at the hospital and a police investigation was started.

Somebody had hurt Baby girl, possibly Big girl as well.

I sat and recalled my movements over the last week with the police. Everyone that had been in contact with the girls was questioned. Except, they weren't. There were other adults present in the house they had been watched in, only HIS cousin had said the girls had never left her sight. Despite the fact she wasn't with either of them when I had entered her house.

I was devastated, my poor little angels. Never again would they leave my side. One hour was all it took. One poxy hour of driving lesson, my sweet innocent babies.

Upon further medical examinations it was concluded that only Baby girl had been hurt. But still the cousin maintained she had always had eyes on them. I couldn't stand to be anywhere near her, or anyone likely to stand up for her. So I asked my Dad if we could go stay with him. He agreed and we left to stay with my Dad in Luton.

# Part Two

Twenty one and faced with Realities

## Broken home

Life became quite blurry. Everything was bittersweet. On the one hand being back with my family was a blessing but on the other hand the awful circumstances that led us to being there weighed ever present on my mind.

I was hyper focused on the happiness and wellbeing of my babies.

Due to the nature of what had occurred it was necessary for social services to be involved. We had attended a child protection conference back in Newcastle and the girl's had been placed on the child protection register. This was until such time as they were satisfied myself and HE were not to blame for the injury.

During that first meeting, information had been shared about HIM that I had not previously been privy to. It was quite serious and the fact that HE had never told me was concerning.

I tried not to dwell on it. My energies were all ploughed into the girls. HE however chose to focus on that more than anything else. We received a paper copy of the initial report and minutes from that conference in the post. HE didn't like the fact that it wasn't stated that HE had been found not guilty at trial. So that became HIS mission.

HE left Luton. HE left his daughters at a time they could benefit from a strong and present Daddy. HE allegedly slept in HIS car as HE visited HIS past Lawyers to have it acknowledged in writing that although charged, HE was found not guilty of rape.

To be honest I didn't care at that point. HE said it was because HE wanted to prove to me that it wasn't true. But I was going through the motions anyway. HE could have told me that HE only had weeks to live and it wouldn't have registered.

I was just getting on with being Mumma.

Big girl loved being at Gandalf's, it was a nice big house for her to play in. She got to see her aunties and Nanny. My girls were OK.

Things settled into a new way of being. I found a local church that housed a mother and toddler group, there was a small soft play section just inside the doors, so I let the girls play whilst I read a few leaflets.

I chatted with another Mumma, she asked the reason for our move, somehow the whole sorry saga of the last few months came tumbling out of my mouth. I hadn't learned or practiced perfunctory responses, the truth spilled.

I told her that I had popped in to try and join the Mum's and Toddler group and that I had been placed on the waiting list. She excused herself, a few minutes later she returned with the news that the Girls and I could join the next Wednesday's session. She was one of the organisers and had bumped us up to the top of the list. I cried with joy. Such a kind gesture. It would herald the beginning of self worth and realisations. But for now it meant the girlies had new friends to make, fun new toys to play with and Mumma got to talk to other Mumma's.

Wednesday rolled around. I had been terrified, but we had so much fun, I didn't want the session to be over. That was one day a week taken care .

On the other days we went to the park, to my Nan's, we went swimming a few times with Nanny. I loved that. She had been a swimming teacher and the fact she had the chance to share that love of water with her great grandchild was amazing to me. Baby girl clung to me in the shallow pool, blew some bubbles, kicked her little legs furiously. Big girl wanted to go in the main pool, because she wasn't a baby. She was so precocious, I loved watching her personality flourish.

A few weeks into Mum's and Tots I discovered there was a preschool just next door in the grounds of the High school. I gave them a call and arranged to go for a visit with Big girl. She loved it, so I signed her up.

Tuesday and Thursday afternoons for starters. My babies were blooming.

I had started making friends with a couple of the Mum's from the toddler group. We went on days out, I popped round theirs with the girls. Life was resembling that of a normal Mumma on the outside. I hadn't felt that happy in years. I finally felt accepted somewhere.

Social Services meetings were still necessary but the new social worker seemed confident that they would be removed from the register at the next conference. There had been no further incidents, the injury had healed, it was pretty clear the danger had passed and I was protecting my girls.


I can't really remember what HE was doing with himself at this point. I can remember that one evening I wanted to try and do something special, act like a married couple. I planned a meal, my Dad and sister's were going to be out. I cleared it with HIM first, HE agreed. So once I had put the girls to bed I cooked a meal, set the table all fancy. I'd found a movie we could watch together. All in all it should have been a nice evening.

When HE was forty five minutes late, I called HIM, HE said HE wouldn't be long.

Another hour passed, I called HIM again. Just leaving, HE had said.

Dad came home, ate his evening meal and went up to bed, still no HIM. HIS phone now just rang out. But HE had only been at the local, closing time had been and gone. I put on my coat and walked round. There was a party going on, the doors were closed, but I could see HIM. I felt so sad, so let down. I was trying to fix things, I was trying to glue us back together. I wanted to feel love, I wanted to show love. HE couldn't care less. More interested in the pub and the people inside it. I sat on a wall outside and sobbed. HE came over, shouted at me for showing HIM up. Never mind the special meal HE had agreed to and not shown up for. I was wrong. I walked home alone and went to bed. Watched my sleeping babies. They deserved more than this.

Dad's tenancy was up, we had to move out. We approached the council and were placed in temporary accommodation. Which is a privately rented property via the council until a permanent council property becomes available. It was awful. No heating, single glazing, dirty, mouse infested in an undesirable part of town. But it was a roof over our heads and at that moment there was nothing more I could do than to make the best of it.

I had picked up driving lessons again. I really needed to pass my test. The new house was a two mile uphill walk away from preschool and Mum's and Tots.

I enrolled myself in the local college. Thought I could do something for myself, give myself the ability to earn money because HE wasn't. I wanted more from life than sitting on benefits. I chose something that I could easily do from home and around the girls commitments. It was one day per week. A couple of times HE wasn't home in time in the morning and I ended up being late.

The more time I spent with other Mum's, other people, the deeper the realisation that my marriage was beyond saving. My beautiful girls were growing more aware of things. They noticed his absence. Other little kids would play Mummy's and Daddy's, my angel's played Mum's and Darlings. It was cute, but sad in equal measure. A family unit we were not. Well the girls and I were. So I came to a decision and asked HIM to leave.

A few months passed, I planned a surprise party for my Dad's 50th, which I later learned that he hated.

Life was a new kind of normal, My girls and I against the world. We went about our days with less anxiety. I felt lighter, happier. I still carried a modicum of guilt. I had failed at being grown up, had quit on my vows.

HE started begging for us to be a family again. Promised to be more active with the girls, pay more attention. I had an image of my little girls playing with Daddy, Daddy reading them stories. I was waning. Then HE sold it. HE said that if we got back together we could have a baby. HE knew how much I wanted a boy. So I relented. Marriage was back on.

## Happiness

I had been contacting the council weekly in an effort to be moved somewhere better as our living arrangement just wasn't good enough. Every morning that we spent in council waiting rooms I would try to spin into a mini adventure. We would take story books to read, colouring books, also the girls quite enjoyed playing with toys that were in the corner of the waiting room.

They never knew why we were there and were quite content with their distractions. Eventually I had been placed on a scheme that meant if I found a privately rented property, the council would cover the cost of any deposit. It was a way for them to lower the number of registered homeless and ease the enormous pressure in housing allocations that they had. The hunt was on. It didn't take me long.

We moved into a three bedroom terrace with a garden, closer to the town centre and nearer to the preschool.

The girls loved how much space we now had, I bought them a swing set for the garden. This place actually felt like a home.

Play dates, pre school, Mums and Tots continued. I was driving by now so getting from a to b had become a lot less complicated.

It wasn't long before it was time for Big girl to begin Primary school. She moved up with many of her little friends from preschool.

I remember her first day, her sandy blonde hair tied in pig tails, navy pinafore on. So grown up, yet so tiny at the same time. She was understandably excited, the stream of animated conversation never halted for a second.

Baby girl gave Big girl a huge squeeze, waved her sister goodbye as we walked out of the school yard. As we reached the gate I turned, there was Big girl. She had decided that she wasn't ready for school after all and she wanted to come to Nanny's house with Mumma.

I took her hand, led her back inside, gave her a reassuring hug and promised to be right at the front of all the other Mumma's at pick up time. She settled very quickly after that.

Baby girl and I started attending Stay and Play sessions in the Family Room at Big girls school. I also started volunteering at Mum's and Tot's . Then came time for Baby girl to start preschool. Our schedules were filling up. We three Girlies were settled and fulfilled.

Then I discovered I was pregnant. My joy along with my belly began to grow.

A few months into the pregnancy, my Nan suffered a devastating stroke.

She was in hospital for a few months. I would visit her twice a day most days, making sure I was there for meal times so that I could feed her. I took home her washing and made sure she was as comfortable and felt as loved as could be. The girls had completed every puzzle in the day room and would push each other around on a wheeled Zimmer frame. The young nurses always had a smile for my little beauties.

As the weeks progressed Nanny grew stronger, she began physio, her speech became less slurred, it was small progress but a little piece of Nanny was returning.

Unfortunately she became unwell having been struck down with C.Diff. (Clostridium Difficile)

So physio halted as she was placed in isolation in a side room. It was very frustrating, she had so been enjoying the physio, now she was confined to bed again and her progress reversed. Her mood dipped. I tried my hardest to keep her upbeat. The infection cleared, it was time for her to go home.

My Dad had built a temporary wall in her living room to create two rooms, so her bed space was separate from her living area. Carers were employed to tend to her hygiene needs. I had offered to do it myself, but she refused. I could understand her reasons, she had always been fiercely independent, this was her worst nightmare.

I would still visit everyday. Make sure to get her washing all done, wash any dishes, make her meals. She had taken to staying in a reclining chair day and night. She had fallen out of the bed and preferred to stay where she couldn't be dropped. It wasn't right for her at all. She would slip or feel as though she were slipping at night. I would receive a frantic phone call in the middle of the night saying she was slipping, would rush round to help. There were days I would be travelling backwards and forwards upwards of four times per day. She needed more security, I was worried for her constantly.

# Four becomes Six

I had an idea that perhaps we should live together, that way the help was only a room away. Her house was sold and we moved into a larger property with two reception rooms. She had the front room as her room, but the idea was she could be transferred into her wheelchair to join us in the living room or garden when she wished.

So now home consisted of myself, Nanny, Big girl, Baby girl and HIM. Although as before HE was never really present.

Quite soon after we moved in, adult social services set the wheels in motion on an extension for Nanny. It would include a wet room with a ceiling mounted hoist. It would make her life a lot more bearable. She had not long been told that any further physio was pointless and she was resigned to immobility for life. So the promise of this new extension had been just the pick me up she needed.

I tried so often to encourage her to come into the garden with the girls and I, she would always resist, saying it was too much hassle. Perhaps if the new room opened straight into the garden she would be more inclined to roll out with us. She had always loved sitting outside before the stroke, she enjoyed watching the birds.

We had several meetings over the following few months, an architect came out, went away to draw it all up. Nanny finally had a little spark back in her eyes.

At the same time we were preparing for baby number three. Unfortunately walking became painful, I had developed a condition called Symphysis Pubis Dysfunction, basically it meant that the ligaments around my hips had loosened too much making the area very uncomfortable. Things at home became quite tricky. But I ploughed on.

I had booked a gender scan in Milton Keynes as the hospital in Luton had a blanket ban on revealing gender. Big girl was going to come along with us, she was very excited to meet her new baby sibling.

It was such a lovely experience, far nicer than the fluorescent lit hospital scans. It was warm and welcoming, like somebody's cosy front room. The lady put the gel on and I explained to Big girl what was happening, she eagerly watched the screen. I will never forget the smile that spread across her face as she finally saw her Baby brother in super high tech 4D. The Lady printed us off some pictures and handed an envelope to Big girl with My Baby Brother written on the front and her own set of photos inside.

A slight issue with baby boy's kidneys had shown up, not anything to be overly concerned about just something for the hospital to keep an eye on.

We headed home, I was elated and so excited to meet my baby boy. We told Baby girl that she was getting a little brother, she did a happy dance around the room. Such bliss in those moments. HE seemed happy as well. Maybe HE would take more of an interest in a male child.

Things progressed and due to my condition I was booked into be induced two weeks early.

I was dropped off early in the morning, I had a book to read, some fizzy pop as that was my craving and I settled in.

To be honest it was nice to have a bit of a relax, yes the inserting of the gel and prodding around was annoying but at that point, to lay on a bed with my feet up, my book for company and no interruptions, was heaven.

Two lots of gel hadn't helped , labour just wasn't happening. I was transferred up to the maternity ward into a side room. HE came to visit, seemed annoyed that I wasn't in labour yet, then left. I couldn't have any more gel as having previously had a caesarean there was a risk the scar could rupture. So other options were being discussed.

It was decided upon that my waters would be manually broken to get things moving. A Dr came in to break them but failed after a couple of attempts, he just succeeded in hurting me. I was left to sleep for a while before being taken into a delivery suite and hooked up to a drip with some drug or other to speed things along. I noticed a bubble in the cannula, I pointed it out to the midwife but she was sure it was fine. Nothing was happening. I felt sure that labour should have at least started by now.

The midwife came back in once HE had returned, she noticed that the drip hadn't gone down at all, she jiggled the cannula, the air bubble vanished , from that point forwards it was game on. At around 7 am on the twelfth of August my long awaited perfect little boy made his entrance into the world. He honestly looked like a teeny tiny grumpy old man. I loved him, my perfect boy. We were taken back up to the side room, HE went home. Baby boy and I took the time to get to know one another. I soaked in every delicious second, those tiny breaths, the rise and fall of his teeny chest. My heart swelled. His Sister's were going to absolutely adore him.

Their excited faces as they crept into the room later that day were a picture. They came straight to me for a cuddle, eyes darting around distractedly. I kissed them both before introducing them to their baby brother. They both beamed with pride, wanted to take him home straight away. I explained to them that we would both have to stay in hospital overnight but that we would be home tomorrow. They grew a little downcast, but perked up when I promised that once home they could give him cuddles. They tenderly kissed his forehead, told him that they loved him and waved goodbye.

## Responsibilities

I was so glad to get baby boy home. I had this vision of quietly settling him in, squeezes with my girlies.

HE opened the door, I sat down, I was still quite sore, the girls sat beside me and then HE announced HE was going out. To wet the baby's head. I was suddenly very overwhelmed. I was in pain, had a new-born, my girlies and Nanny to suddenly take care of. I tried my absolute hardest to swallow the lump in my throat. I asked if HE had to go that night, if perhaps HE could wait a night or so. HE said HE couldn't let HIS friends down, then left.

I hobbled into Nanny's room, laid Baby on her chest so they could meet, before popping him down for a nap in his Moses basket. I made a quick tea for Nanny and the girls, basic but filling. Bath time was quickly upon us, baby needed a feed, the carers arrived to change Nanny into her bed things. The girls were growing ratty, bath time was overdue, it was now bedtime. I sat there with baby firmly attached, pretty helpless in that moment, tears pricked my eyes. This was the first day home, HE should be here to get the girls to bed, to bond with his new son. Not propping up a bar with his mates. I tried to call HIM, to ask for help, it went straight to voicemail.

Why was I such an idiot. Why did I think it would be any different. My Babies were my everything. I managed to get the girls to bed albeit late and minus the bath. I needed to get it clear in my head, normal was me, my three babies, Nanny and the occasional surly man milling about. Any ideas of sharing burdens was gone. Reality was it was all down to me. His contribution was making Nan her Weetabix and a cup of tea in the mornings, which she would leave untouched until I returned from the school run to sort her pills.

At times it was too much, I did need help. If baby boy was having a particularly needy day, nothing else would get done. Well not nothing, but priorities had to be determined. HE was always out or in HIS shed. If it had been work, it would have been ok, I was simply fulfilling the woman's role, but it wasn't. It was smoking weed in the shed or round his friend's playing PlayStation in their bedrooms or getting off his face in the pub. Not exactly the life a married Dad of three should have been living. I felt ashamed. Fortunately I never really had that long to sit and ruminate. Any nice gesture I would cling to the hope that change was afoot.

I threw myself into caring for the four most important people in my life.

When baby boy was only twelve weeks old I discovered that I was pregnant again. I was pleased that he would have a friend close in age like the girls, but I was simultaneously terrified. I struggled on some days as it was already, how on earth would I cope with another baby? I pushed the doubts to one side and carried on.

Baby girl was now in reception year of primary school, Big girl was in year two, so Mum's and tots, stay and play sessions it was just myself and Baby boy. I had a new circle of Mum friends as well as the established. Since we had moved into the house with Nanny I had forged a good friendship with a lady down the street whose children attended the same school. We would swap school runs, watch each other's children, borrow tin openers as well as the obvious cups of tea and chats. I actually received more practical day to day help and support from her than I did my own Husband.

She would quite often come up and borrow baby boy, she would pop up to borrow something and take him back down with her. I quite liked my life at that time. I was busy but fulfilled by my babies and my friends.

As this the fourth pregnancy progressed the issue with my hips returned with a vengeance. Climbing the stairs became unbearable. Meanwhile baby boy was hitting all his milestones, little words, walking. He was my little ball of cuteness. Big blue eyes. He was gorgeous, so were my girls, I felt so lucky.

Life for Nanny wasn't so good. The council had decided that they weren't going to build the extension after all. This absolutely devastated her. She had spent months talking of it, imagining, looking forward, then her dreams just dashed, for no apparent reason. Her overall health deteriorated. She was in and out of hospital with seemingly insignificant issues, but due to her underlying conditions they posed a greater risk. I wanted so much to make her happy. I just really didn't know how to. She just seemed to have lost any semblance of a zest for life.

After one hospital stay, the transport had brought her home and placed her in the armchair in her room, we asked her if she would prefer to go straight into bed, but she was happy to wait for the evening carers. Once the children were in bed I sat down with and we watched the soaps she had come to enjoy together, whilst I filled her in on all the happenings she had missed whilst in hospital. The soaps finished and we were both getting tired, I wondered where her carers were.

At around 10pm, which was three hours late a carer arrived. It took two carer to operate the hoist. Unwilling to call for assistance the carer assured us that she was capable of operating it alone. I made it clear that at eight and a half months pregnant I really wasn't able to assist with any lifting. Again she assured us it was fine and she had it under control.

Very disappointingly, she hadn't remotely got it under control. Half way between the bed and the chair, Nanny fell out of the hoist and onto the floor! She had dropped her! Remember Nanny was completely paralysed on the left side, there was no way she could get up from there. She was also a tall lady, Five feet ten, the carer a mere five three at most.

I was absolutely furious, but Nanny needed help. I couldn't help. I was hardly able to walk at that time, I hobbled as quickly as I could to the back door, the shed was too far, I couldn't walk there, I picked up a stone and launched it at the shed to get HIS attention.

HE came raging out of the door screaming and shouting, I pleaded with HIM to come and help Nanny, which HE did, But I was still in the bad books for having smashed the shed window.

I made Nanny an Ovaltine and sat with for a while longer to make sure she was comfortable and that the ordeal hadn't traumatised her too much. She was fine, just happy to be back in bed. The next day I put in a complaint to the caring company.

## Not so secret Seven

The Caesarean was drawing closer whilst my relationship with HIM was getting worse. HIS involvement in everything family related was met with disdain. It was as though we were in HIS way, keeping HIM from something important. If HE ever actually came to the park with us after a paltry ten minutes HE would insist on leaving, because HE was bored. Never mind that the children were having fun, HIS happiness was far more relevant.

After a particularly tough day, where I had needed help, walking was painful to the point of tears. I asked my friend down the street to watch the children for an hour whilst I tried to talk to HIM, I hobbled to the shed to express how I felt. Instead of understanding I was met with anger and insults. I fell to the floor exhausted with it all and sobbed, I screamed at HIM for being so utterly selfish, HE called me crazy. I stood up and somehow through sheer rage I ran inside and up the stairs. I collapsed at the top of the stairs in agony. I had been bumping up the stairs backwards for weeks as I was unable to climb them, yet I had just ran up them. I had never felt pain like it.

My Dad came round to sit with the children whilst HE took me to the hospital.

They checked me over, it wasn't labour. My hip had popped out and so every time baby moved it sent searing pain through my pelvis. I was given pain relief and booked in for the first caesarean the next morning.

Seven thirty the next morning they pulled Baby Boy number two out into the world. They cleaned him up and checked him over whilst the doctors tied my tubes, sterilising me.

We moved into recovery, HE went home.

My new beautiful boy and I were alone. He wasn't very happy bless him, he'd been crying since the theatre. I'd tried feeding him, thought maybe he was hungry . He wasn't remotely interested in taking the breast. I asked the midwife if I could try him with some formula, she brought in a bottle and for the first time since he was born, Baby boy was content. What a perfect creature. I savoured every second.

We had been on the ward a few hours when HE came with the other kiddies. They came in eating a McDonalds, I was so hungry, I got my hopes up thinking a yummy burger was coming my way. But I had nothing.

The girls absolutely loved Baby boy, big boy seemed confused. He was sat on the bed with me, at just eleven months old he was still a baby himself, I cuddled him and made sure that he knew he was still loved and important. A nurse called to the bed with regards baby boys TB shot, HE wasn't happy that I had given the go ahead without consulting HIM first. I tried reminding HIM that the children's immunisations had always been up to date due to my taking them and that HE had never showed interest before. I was told off, when tears pricked my eyes I was called pathetic before HE took the older three home.

I laid with my new angel, listened to the other Mumma's on the ward. Some young, some older, some brand new to motherhood and unsure. I enjoyed listening to their interactions with the Daddies. Although sad that my own babies had a Daddy that didn't really give a hoot, I felt pleased for those I came across that had what mine lacked.

In the bed opposite was the wife of one of my best friends from childhood. I hadn't seen him in years, was a strange place for a catch up but nice none the less.

Baby Boy and I were cleared to leave. I packed up our stuff and awaited HIS arrival. I watched as other families left. Daddies beaming with pride carrying their new bundles whilst the Mumma's walked by their side.

HE rang, told me to go down. I had Baby boy, a big bag and was two days post op from major surgery, I told HIM this, HE insisted

HE couldn't park. I relayed this to the midwife and as I suspected I couldn't leave without them having eyes on an appropriate car seat. I called HIM back to tell HIM this, I was shouted at.

My friend from school was sat with his wife, could hear me being shouted at, I was so embarrassed. He offered to carry my bag down for me, but I knew how that would be perceived by HIM and declined. I explained to the midwife, she came down in the lift with me carrying the bag. I thanked her, got in the car immediately downcast. Back to reality.

Summer holidays were fast upon us. Mum's and Tot's had a special summer meet that we could take the older kids to. I was unable to drive for six weeks following the caesarean so I strapped the boys into the double buggy and the girls and I walked over with my friend from down the street. All the kiddies had so much fun, Baby boy enjoyed all the fuss reigned upon him.

We filled the summer days with walks to the park, there were two parks local enough to walk, the hills back home were killer with a double buggy but was great for my post baby body.

I wished summer could last forever. Yes it was hard work, but seeing all four of my babies bonding with each other, having so much fun together, it was great.

I wasn't really paying attention to the marriage at this point, I had resigned myself to getting on with it. I took care of Nanny as best as I could whilst singlehandedly tending to all the kids. There was a stage I was existing on three hours of broken sleep a night. Baby boy would still wake for a feed through the night, big boy was teething and Nan had become very confused. She never seemed to realise the difference between night and day. She would shout out at all hours, request a cup of tea or ask random questions. She also cried out in pain a lot or wanted her leg pulled.

By now our bedroom was an attic room with just a wooden ladder, so I would be up and down ladder and the staircase continuously every night, all night long. If it hadn't been so tiring it would have been comical. I felt as though I was living in a comedy sketch stuck on repeat for months. Caffeine pills were my very best friend. I must have looked horrendous.

The most annoying factor though was that in spite of all this HE would still take himself for a nap near enough every day. HE would come in from the shed high as a kite and swan off for a nap, during which time I had to ensure the children were quiet.

If I dared to question HIM or mention how tired I was I would be fobbed off with the promise of a lay in or how he would get up through the night that evening. Neither of those things ever happened. If I became exasperated I would be accused of being unreasonable and a row would erupt.

I'm the type of angry that needs time out to calm down. So the times HE would rage, I would try to leave the house. I would be attempting to go for a walk to clear my head. This wasn't allowed, HE would physically stop me. Once HE grabbed my wrist so hard that it was sprained from trying to wriggle free. I had it strapped up for a while and took heavy pain killers. Another time HE chased me down the street and threw me over his shoulder, carried me back in. One incident when I tried to get away in the car, HE yanked open the door and took out the keys. I was quite literally trapped.

I told HIM that I didn't love him, that I wanted to split. I had had enough, this wasn't a relationship, it was just ridiculous. After much pleading on HIS part HE agreed to leave, but only on the condition that HE could take Baby girl with him. It was bonkers. I refused. But HE went over my head and asked her directly. Did she want to go with Daddy to Newcastle to stay with Nanna, to see her cousins. It sounded like a big adventure to her.

So HE packed and they both left in the car.

Big girl and I sat together on the sofa and sobbed. Not for HIM, for baby girl. Big boy didn't understand, he just gave us both big cuddles, baby boy was oblivious.

A few hours later HE came back. HE couldn't do it, HE drove so far and realised that HE just couldn't, pulled over. Baby girl was confused, Big girl and I held her tight.

The girls went to bed, I settled the boys, HE wanted to explain.

I didn't want HIM there. I was done. HE cried, spun me a tale about having been abused by a cousin as a kid, how HE couldn't go back to Newcastle as HE would kill the cousin. Quite why it had never stopped HIM being there before I did not know. I told HIM that I didn't care, that we were done, HE had to leave. HE cried HIMSELF to sleep on the sofa. Crocodile tears probably.

HE decided that HE would get a place in Luton so that HE could still see the kids. Pretty ironic seeing as HE currently lived with them and never spent any time with them.

HE said Baby girl was going with HIM. I put my foot down, said she was absolutely not. HE claimed it would only be on paper so that the council would house HIM.

Unfortunately for him HE needed a letter from my Nan stating that they could no longer live there, she refused to put Baby girl on the letter. So HE ended up staying on the sofa.

I made an appointment with a solicitor and started the process for a divorce. I needed nine counts of unreasonable behaviour, easy.

I was focused. I was twenty five, I may well have had four kids but I was young enough to start again, to find eventual happiness. It would be so much easier without HIM.

One evening my friend down the road suggested we go out out. So we both got all poshed up and together with another Mum in the street we hit the town centre. We had a great time. Ordinarily on a night out I would be distracted by my phone all night long with constant texts and calls from HIM checking up on me. That night, HE was not my problem, I ignored my phone. It turned into a late night and at 4am another call came through, this time I answered. I was screamed at for being irresponsible, told if I wasn't home within half an hour HE was packing all the kids up in the car and taking them to Newcastle, I would never see them again. I went home.

The riot act was read, thoroughly. Whilst hypocrisy is amusing in hindsight, in that moment I felt like the worst Mumma. Not due to my night out, the kids were sound asleep, they would know no different if I had arrived home at midnight. It was HIM, HIS threats.

HE was going to wake them up, tell my little girls, aged five and six, that Mumma was a slut. That Mumma would rather be out all night shagging random blokes than be with them. It was so far from the truth. But I felt immense guilt for saddling them with a Daddy that could think of hurting them in that way. All I had ever wanted was a happy family. A Mumma and a Daddy that loved each other and their smiling happy babies. I had never got that with HIM and I never would. That night passed by without him actively waking the girls, although his shouts had stirred them and they do remember that.

HE continued to sleep on the sofa, spending the odd night at a friends. I wished HE would just do one.


My Dad was decorating my hallway, I had settled to watch a movie in the living room as all babies and Nan were settled. HE decided to watch it with me. HE sat beside me on the sofa, I moved to widen the space between us, HE edged closer. I tried to wriggle further down but had run out of sofa. HE put HIS hand on my leg, told me how much HE loved me. I felt so sick, so utterly stuck, I had split with HIM months before, why was HE even there, the world was closing in , I felt suffocated, I had no escape.

The next thing I was aware of was a paramedic standing in my living room and I was leaning on my Dad still on the sofa. HE was crying. Apparently I had suffered a panic attack and HE had thought I was dying.

I had suffered them as a teenager, I popped to the GP the next day and was prescribed some beta blockers to take should I feel overly anxious again. What I really needed was for my suddenly present Husband to disappear.

## Poorly Girlie

Christmas and New Year passed by without too much fuss from me. I was forever busy with making sure all my little people and Nanny were content and catered to.

February arrived and brought snow with it. The girls had a thoroughly good time rolling around making snow angels, snowball fighting and of course the obligatory snowman building, Big boy had a little turn as well.

These were the moments. What it was all about.

I brought them all in and gave them an early bath. As I was drying them I noticed a rash on Baby girl. I got a glass from downstairs to check as is hammered into you by health visitors.

The rash stayed bright red under the pressure from the glass. I made sure everyone was dressed and warm before informing HIM that she needed to see a DR as soon as possible. I stayed with boys and Big girl while HE took baby girl to an out of hours DR.

HE brought her home about an hour later with a prescription for antihistamines, was told it was an allergic reaction. I didn't really buy that explanation, but found a 24 hour pharmacy and gave her a dose before she slept.

The next morning the rash was worse, was spreading. I asked my friend to take Big girl to school, I took Baby girl to an emergency appointment at our usual GP's.

He took one look at her and started writing a letter for the hospital, I was to take her immediately to the Assessment Ward, he suspected she had Henoch Schonlein Purpura, a rare disease which if left untreated could escalate rapidly. The rash was in fact blood vessels that had burst, it was steadily getting worse and her legs were beginning to swell. I rushed to the hospital, they ran the appropriate tests before confirming that the GP's suspicion was correct. It was HSP.

Besides monitoring her there wasn't much they could do, the tests showed that thankfully there were no serious affects. So we went home with a prescription of steroids and hope that the inflammation would reverse. Her joints continued to swell, but she seemed ok. She was a very bubbly and lively little girl, so whilst a little muted than usual, she seemed fine.

That was until 3am. I heard her cry out, thought she had just had a night time accident, which wasn't unusual, but then I heard big girl scream in terror, I quickened my pace and ran in their room. Baby girl was vomiting violently, but now I understood Big girls terror, it was Blood she was bringing up. I had to get her to hospital. I cleaned her up, tried to reassure both girls that everything would be ok. I was quite good at containing my panic in times like this, it called for calm and positive action, a crying Mumma would make matters far more scary.

I called HIM to watch Big girl and raced up to the hospital. We had open access to the ward so headed straight there, no messing about. I pushed her up to the ward in a single buggy, she had a bowl on her lap as she was still vomiting.

They seemed more concerned this time. Stuck a drip in her and ordered scans.

Eventually the vomiting subsided and she was moved into a side ward. I read her stories to take her mind off things, gave her a sense of adventure about it all. The scan results came back all clear, the concern was that her bowel was twisting but thankfully the blood had simply been due to the steroids and the effect on her stomach lining. So they were stopped. She was kept in overnight for observation to make sure her vitals all returned back to normal.

For some reason HE had decided that she was dying and had got HIS brother and Mother down from Newcastle to say goodbye. It was a scary experience, but at no point was it suggested she was in mortal danger. Once the drip had taken effect, the consultant was happy for her to come home.

Her joints were so swollen though, I had to but her a pair of fluffy slip on boots, three sizes larger than her normal size. She couldn't wait to get back to school to tell all her friends about the night she nearly died. I informed the teachers that she may be more tired than usual, that she was swollen, not contagious and gave them some paracetamol in case she complained of pain. She coped amazingly. She was proud that she had fat legs and was allowed to wear brown boots to school. I had brought home some urine strip tests from the hospital, I was to dip her urine once a week , if they were high in either blood or protein I was to take her back in. Thankfully though I never needed to. HSP caused no further issues. All signs of rash disappeared, her legs returned to the normal size, life continued.

The next few months were quite busy. Boys were growing, progressing, basically being awesome little boys. The girls continued to be little superstars, I was still very much enjoying being a busy Mumma on the go. I don't really remember if HE and I were together at that time, HE wasn't around, but occasionally pops up in a memory. I was honestly that busy.

# Time for Goodbyes

Nanny started needing more time and attention. Her needs became more time consuming. Her catheter kept coming out somehow. Every couple of days it would come out and her bed was drenched. The district nurses must have grown weary of my constant calls. She became more depressed. The Dr upped her anti depressant, it didn't really seem to make any difference in her mood. I think the fact she existed in her very worst nightmare was more the issue, unfortunately that wasn't something anyone could solve.

She stopped eating her meals, would just outright refuse them. I got her some ensure, a meal replacement shake designed to get the necessary vitamins etc in to people either unwilling or unable to eat regular food. Problems just seemed to keep mounting up.

I remember being in tears trying to encourage her to eat her weetabix, as silly as that seems, I would put some of her medication in the weetabix as she struggled to swallow them otherwise. I had been finding pills in her bed and on the floor in her room for weeks. She was giving up. She didn't want food and she didn't want her pills.

I pulled the GP aside after a home visit, explained how she hadn't been taking all her meds and that I wasn't sure what to do. Nanny had stated that she no longer wanted to be taken to hospital as she was sick of it and wanted to be at home when she died. She asked to see my Mum, so Mum flew over from Spain. Together with my Mum and I Nanny planned her funeral, she decided which songs she wanted, who was to be invited, what we would eat.

I remember falling onto the floor whilst washing her sheets one day, the reality that she was dying and actively wanted to had suddenly hit me. Even though the Nanny that had been my constant, my go to, my confidante and cheerleader all these years had pretty much been swallowed up by the stroke, she was still here. Glimmers of the woman she had been still showed up sometimes. My heart was breaking with the reality that sooner rather than later even that would be gone. No more Nanny, The end.

I sat on the kitchen floor, sheets half in and half out of the washer and I sobbed. Big, loud, painful sobs.

Then she called out to me. I shoved the sheets in the dryer and went in to see her. I wiped my tears and hugged her. She was growing so weak, I didn't want to squeeze too hard in case I broke her. She said it was fine, I hugged her as tight as I dare, having a little cry into her shoulder.

She asked me what was wrong. I told her nothing, shrugged it off, told her I loved her. She told me she was proud of me, that I was a good Mumma, that she was sorry to be a burden. I told her to shut up, I loved her, that we look after those we love and she wasn't a burden. She told me to be happy, I said I'd try, she told me that wasn't good enough, that I wasn't to try, I was to do.


Big girl was turning seven. She was having a picnic party. I had made her and her little friends picnic bags, filled with sandwiches and treats, we all took a walk to the park behind our house, they played in the park and ate their picnic before we headed back up to the house for party games and birthday cake. Their collective favourite was pin the sunglasses on Hannah Montana. Full tummies and smiley faces all around. I had a very happy little girl. It was a nice reprieve from the seriousness of the last few months.


The following week Nanny stopped eating all together. She was refusing medication, began hallucinating, babbling nonsensically and her cries of pain grew louder. I had to pour oral morphine into her mouth a few times per day in an effort to just make things more bearable for her. I rang my Auntie, explained that I thought she was probably nearing the end so she travelled down to spend some time with her.

Every day was now a routine of painting on a smile with the children, making sure all their needs were tended to whilst fretting that I wasn't spending enough time with Nanny.

My aunt sat with her, she could sense it as well. It was close.

One evening my auntie had left to stay at her hotel, asked me to call if there was any change. That night I sat up with Nanny the whole night.

She asked for cuddles a few times, shouted random words, called out for her Mum and had a conversation with the man in the hat.

Around five thirty a.m she told me to go to bed, I refused. She told me I was being silly, that she was fine, she loved me and that I needed to sleep, I asked her if she was sure.

I told her that I loved her and that if she needed me to call out. I nipped upstairs and laid on the sofa.

At around six thirty Baby girl came in, she had been downstairs and she said Nanny hadn't moved when she said good morning.

I ran downstairs. She must have waited for me to leave her alone. She was gone.

I wiped her face, cleaned her up a bit, kissed her cheek then called my Auntie and a Dr.

A locum called round to confirm and record the death.

Just like that my world was changed forever. No more Nanny.

That day was a blur of phone calls and preparations. My Dad took the girls out so that they weren't around when the undertakers came to take her body.

I let them in, showed them to her room and sat on the stairs as they shut the door behind themselves. I could hear them bumping around, moving furniture around and transferring her. They wheeled her out on a gurney, I watched as they put her body into the back of the private ambulance and drove away.

The house suddenly felt so empty. She was gone. In spirit and now her physical body.

The following weeks were a jumbled blur. My Auntie attended the initial appointment with the undertakers, we arranged the funeral date, some basic requests, sorted the announcement for the newspaper.

I paid one last visit to Nanny's body. I genuinely felt like laughing. They had dressed her in a frilly pink nightgown with a high lacy collar. She abhorred pink and most things girly. I could almost hear her grumbling about how they had made her look all dainty and daft. She seemed peaceful, but I couldn't feel her. Whatever it was that made her Nanny, was absent.

This was just the body she steered through life in. The body that had grown her three children, that gave the best most reassuring hugs, the body that had experienced all the high points and suffered all the lows for it's seventy three years.

I felt relief for her mostly. She had hated what her life had become after the stroke.

I had tried to make things as comfortable as I could for her, but this was a woman that took pride in her independence. She had raised her children as a single parent whilst working full time to support them. She was strong. She had always hated being dependent on anyone for anything, yet in the end she had been, completely. There was nothing she could do for herself. It broke my heart to see her in such a state. Pushing my own feelings of loss aside, I was pleased for her. She no longer had to endure the endless suffering that had been her last years.

## How could You

My Auntie returned to her home, my Mum flew over from Spain.

We began to go through Nanny's things. Photographs were distributed, keepsakes taken, her bed and hoist were returned to the health authority . Her room sat empty, still.

I found myself sitting in the armchair in what had been her room, looking around, reflecting on how I could have been better. My Auntie had been named executor of the will so she was sorting out all the financial arrangements. My Mum came in holding the phone while I was sat in Nan's chair, she handed it to me, it was my Auntie. What she was about to tell me absolutely devastated me.

There had always been around three thousand five hundred pounds left in Nan's account, the monies that went in and were paid out never took away from that total.

But it was gone. The balance was zero. I couldn't understand it. It must be a mistake. But it wasn't a mistake it was an awful truth.

I hadn't had her card for a while, in fact I couldn't recall the last time I'd checked her balance. I had asked HIM for it the week prior to Nan's death in order to pay for the girl's next block of swimming lessons. Nanny had been a swimming instructor, had taught most of Luton to swim during the mid sixties and the seventies. So it had been important for her that the girls learned and she wanted to be the one to pay for that.

I never once spent a penny of her money without consent or instruction directly from her.

I remembered HIS reluctance to hand over the card when I had asked for it. Muttering something about not using it for anything else. It made sense now, well, sort of.

HE had been worried I would check the balance and see that he had stolen all her money.

My Aunt informed me that two hundred and fifty pounds had been taken out on the day she had died.

I felt utterly sick!

How could HE do such a thing? I had known HE was scumbag as HE had been breaking into people's sheds in our street, HE had even burgled the house opposite ours. So the scumminess wasn't a surprise, but stealing from a dying woman, from my Nan.

I hated HIM!

I rang HIM, asked where the money was. HE didn't deny it. I told HIM that HE needed to go away and stay away.

I was so ashamed. The guilt I felt was immeasurable.

I already lived with the shame in knowing HE was a thief. I had tried so many times to get rid of HIM it just never worked, HE clung on like a persistent leech.

Now on top of that shame, coupled with the grief in losing Nanny, I had to live knowing I had let her down. I had brought HIM into her life, I had given HIM access to her bank account. My one consistent source of support since childhood and I had failed her, massively. If I hadn't brought HIM into things, then the money she had made sure was there to cover her funeral costs would still be there. I wanted the ground to open up and swallow me. I was so very lost. There doesn't exist a word descriptive enough to explain the disappointment I felt.

The funeral came and went. The well wishes dried up. I was left in my home. The house that despite my four boisterous children felt cold and empty. The home that we were quite possibly about to lose.

Practicalities of daily life took over the shame. I had babies to love. I felt so alone. I had big decisions to make. The house had to be sold, the money left from the sale after debts paid wasn't enough to buy anything of a similar size in Luton, so moving away seemed the best option.

My mind was absent at that time. I was put on medication to try and alleviate some of the darkness. At some point or other HE came back. I was too broken to fight it, I just went along with things. I was floating through life, an empty shell going through the motions. Babies were cared for, beyond that, I couldn't, there was nothing, just an absence of me.

Fast forward to the house being sold, Wales was decided upon as houses were cheap. Wheels were rolling, a house was purchased, in joint names and off we went.

# Part Three

A Fresh New Life

# Hello Wales

The excitement levels upon moving were palpable. A whole new adventure. The girls had their own bedrooms for the first time, kiddies had a playroom that was to be filled with all their fun things. The garden was a bit of an issue for the boys as there were concrete steps and differing levels, but that just meant that Mumma had to play in the garden with them.

Our house was in a small town in the Neath valley. The house was set back into a hill so we had views of the other side of the valley, vast woodland behind us. It was supposed to be the beginning of a new peaceful existence.

The girls settled into their new school, which was a short walk away. The boys and I found Mum's and toddler groups twice a week. We were establishing ourselves within the community, reaching out, meeting people, things were good. A peace settled in.

HE was looking into training in something, in order to actually go to work. It was more than likely though just a delaying tactic, an excuse once more to not get a job.

As per usual I ploughed all my attentions into the kids. Trying to make new friends, succeeding in entertaining my babies each day. I found lots of fun things for us to do. Although still busy, it felt odd to not have Nanny to care for also.

I missed her so much. I felt immense guilt for being with HIM. But in my weakness I had swallowed HIS excuse and I still felt as HIS wife I had a duty to try and make things right, to keep HIM around so that the children still had their Daddy.

The tale was that HE had been running Cocaine and money backwards and forwards to another part of the country, one evening after a run HE had a gun pulled on HIM, was threatened with death or harm brought upon myself or the children if payment for allegedly stolen drug money wasn't returned.

Coincidentally it amounted to the same sum held in Nan's bank account.

With grief comes a massive vulnerability. I hadn't forgiven, I just tried to push the negative feelings down and move past it. For better or worse, right? Perhaps the better part was to come.

In May we flew to Spain for a holiday, Big girl would turn eight while we were there. HE had always been a nightmare to travel with. It was always just stress and shouting from start to finish. I think this trip became a catalyst of sorts. It was the first time since the move that I had been majorly publicly humiliated by HIM. The fact that HE chose Big girl's birthday to do it, made it all the more potent. Birthdays always were ruined by HIM, it was almost as though HE couldn't stand anyone being happy or centre of attention. I thought though, having endured so much, perhaps HE would allow us to enjoy one holiday, one birthday minus the dramatics. I had been wrong.

# Twilight

We returned home after a fortnight, my ill feeling growing. A darkness I hadn't felt in a while descended. Then it would lift, briefly.

When lifted I was filled by a surging energy, it was like a bouncing ball in my chest waiting to burst out. It was intense, the children had lots of exciting adventures on those days. But without warning, well there may have been triggers but I wasn't consciously aware of them, a deep darkness would envelope me. The desire to hide away from the world became all consuming.

Something was off.

I went to the G.P, was referred for an outpatients appointment with a psychiatrist. The appointment wasn't until October, it was then June, that was four months away.

HE decided that I just needed a break from the kids, HE booked a weeks holiday to Ibiza for the two of us. HIS Mum and an aunt were going to stay at our house with the children.

A few days after Big boy's third birthday we flew out. I was nervous. I didn't particularly want to spend a week with HIM, alone. But that was me being ungrateful.

It was a beautiful place, but the atmosphere was tense. I felt scrutinised, was tip toeing around HIM. Any signs of "weirdness" were pointed out, highlighted. I tried to act normal, to appear to be enjoying myself.

One evening a row erupted, I was drunk but HE wanted to be in the room, I was peckish, had a hankering for some crisps. Apparently crisps had been code for, the man that had smiled at me downstairs' penis. Name calling ensued. I was trapped. More so than usual.

I locked myself in the bathroom and for the first time since my teens I sliced my arm with a razor. I was just trying to release some of the pulsing pressure of my inadequacies, short comings, failures. After repeated bangs and threats to break down the door I unlocked it. HE noticed the blood and all of a sudden HE cared. I wrapped my arm in clean tissue and laid on the bed. HE attempted to apologise, declare love, I was spent.

I softly cried myself to sleep. I just wanted my babies, not HIM.

Once home, I showered my angels in Love. I had missed them so much, a week away from them had been far too long. A day or a night here or there was plenty for me.

HE returned to HIS course, then decided we should all move to Ibiza. Life continued albeit erratically. My mental health was an ever present issue. I tried so many times to get more help, but each time I was told to sit it out, wait for my appointment in October.

Big boy started Nursery. He had to wear a uniform, it was so tiny yet formal. He looked so cute. I kept up appearances at the school and toddler groups. Tried to paint a picture that everything was good. It worked, for a while. There were days though that it became very difficult to hide. Staying home on those days was by far the best option. I told HIM that I was struggling, that I could maybe use some help. I was just chastised for being lazy.

I drove myself to hospital on one occasion as I was starting to scare myself, the intrusive thoughts were becoming too intense to ignore. The crisis team became involved. They gave me some medication, had a chat with me at home, asked me to write a mood diary. I did as I was told.

I had voluntarily stopped driving after that. The images flashing through my mind were overwhelming, I couldn't trust that they wouldn't take over. Again I asked for help from HIM, was shouted down, HE was stressed from all the work on HIS course.

My car had to go in for an MOT, HE asked me to drop it off. I told HIM that I wasn't comfortable driving, HE said it wasn't far, to suck it up and stop being stupid.

I drove to the unfamiliar garage which admittedly wasn't far. I put the boys into their pushchair and tried to find the man in charge. A guy in overalls said that he would take the keys, so I handed them to him then everyone in the garage started laughing. They were making a joke, I had handed the keys to a random bloke that didn't actually work there. I was very confused. It felt as though they were mocking me. I felt a panic attack begin. I tried to make sure everything was legitimate whilst not looking like a paranoid mess, then headed towards home. Tears were pouring from my eyes, I wanted to go home, shut the door, hide from everyone and everything. So I walked to the school to collect the girls early. The receptionist asked why, I shouted that they were my kids and I wanted them home, she could see the tears in my eyes, there was no hiding my distress any longer. She went and gathered them up for me. I thanked her and apologised.

Baby girl hadn't wanted to leave. She was angry with me. I just really needed to get home. She stood her ground, refused to walk out of the gate. I momentarily lost all composure, I grabbed her round her tiny neck with one hand, spat through gritted teeth that we were going home. I dropped my arm, tears grew stronger, we walked home in silence.

Once we were safely inside, I scooped them all up on the sofa, apologised, told them I loved them more than anything, that Mumma was just not feeling well and that maybe cuddles would help us all feel better. We stayed snuggled on the sofa watching movies.

I hadn't hurt or marked Baby girl, I had just scared her and myself. That wasn't right. I shouldn't have done that. I desperately needed help.

After bedtime I once again told HIM that I wasn't right and I needed more help. HE said I was being selfish. That I wasn't the only person to ever feel sad.

The next day I telephoned the crisis team and they called in for a chat. I was informed that I could attend a day unit at the hospital, but I had to find childcare.

I relayed this to HIM, asked if perhaps HE could get HIS Mum down to watch the kids enabling me to get the help I needed from the day unit and still be around in time for tea.

Big fat nope. Not happening. There was nothing wrong with me. I needed to get my priorities straight, how dare I suggest such a thing.

So I carried on.

# Darkness Descending

Dark thoughts growing steadily. Voices screaming at me, telling me how pathetic and weak I was. I saw glowing eyes and pointed teeth snarling behind people's shoulders, mocking me. I had to keep fighting, smiling, being Mumma.

I was growing weaker. I was too weak to fight this.

Another night, another row with HIM.

I ran from the house, downed some alcohol and walked further away.

I had made a friend in the next village over, so I decided to walk there.

As I crossed the road I stopped to watch the river, I saw a body floating, carried along with the current, I looked around, cars passed, they looked, but they didn't see. Everyone always looked, but no one ever saw me. I felt the urge to join the body in the water, to jump, end my pain, sleep forever on the bottom of the surging river.

I fought the compulsion, continued on my journey.

I arrived at my friends as she was putting her son to bed. I helped him to put on his pyjamas and read him a story , just as I had done with own two boys, whilst she saw to her baby.

We then sat in the kitchen, she gave me a glass of something alcoholic and I rambled at her. Trying to make some kind of sense of my thoughts. I'm not sure she realised how lost I had been. I walked back home in the dark. I was screamed at for being reckless, I didn't care. I slept.


A couple of days passed.

I awoke that morning in the same state of stress I had retired the night before. My emotions screaming to be addressed. It was a week day, so HE had left for HIS course at seven thirty, I was in sole charge of preparing all children and getting them to school.

Not the smoothest of tasks even in a great frame of mind. Breakfasts were made and consumed, clothes chosen and put on, it was just shoes and go time.

Baby girl had other ideas. She couldn't find her shoes, they were not on the shoe rack that lived in the porch, she went off to find them, time was ticking by. If I got them to school late, HE would find out and there would be hell to pay. Baby girl reappeared, still without shoes. I had both boys ready to go, pushchair was up and in position. If we didn't leave now, they would definitely be late. Baby girl shouted at me, repeating words she had heard HIM say. I lost my cool, did the unthinkable. I struck Baby girl in the stomach. Immediately I realised the gravity of what I had done. I should not have done that. I don't know why I had. She cried in shock, I joined her, pulled her to me and hugged her tight, apologising through the sobs. I felt so awful. I hadn't marked her, but I categorically should not have done that.

Everybody was now going to be very late. I was terrified.

Stupidly I decided to leave Baby girl home with Baby boy whilst I drove the other two to their schools. Thankfully in the time that it had taken, no more than fifteen minutes they were both fine, sitting munching biscuits absorbed in Scooby Doo as though nothing were amiss. But I knew different, I urgently needed help.

I called HIM, begged HIM to come home so that I could go see a Dr. HE refused.

The rest of the day was filled with baby cuddles, tv and toys.

I made the children their evening meal then the girls head out to play with a friend, boys were happily amusing themselves in the playroom, whilst I pottered around the kitchen cleaning up.

HE came home seething with rage. How dare I call HIM when HE's on HIS course, how could I be so selfish, why do I only ever think of myself. All the while HE was shouting there was a cacophony in my head, some voices agreeing with HIM, others saying HE was the selfish one. I tried explaining to HIM how desperate I was feeling, I was shouted down again. Determined to be heard I picked up a knife. I looked at HIM with a longing to plunge it deep into HIS chest, I heard one of the boys, it broke the urge, I spun around and stabbed the stainless steel baking tray repeatedly whilst a scream escaped my lungs. The knife had gone all the way though several times, goodness knows how. I took the knife, ran upstairs and slumped against my closed bedroom door. I looked down at the knife, a stream of tears blurring my vision, I pushed it down onto my wrist and swept it across. I just wanted the shame and the pain to end. The knife hadn't cut me, it hadn't even left a mark, I tried again, still nothing.

There was a tiny knock on the door, a little voice called out "Mumma".

I quickly hid the knife, opened the door. It was Big boy. My little Mumma's boy. I let him in the room, pulled him onto my lap leaning against the door, I held him close, smelled his perfect head, he hugged me back as I gently sobbed. I sat up a bit higher and as I called an ambulance for myself my beautiful little boy stroked the tears from my face.

This was it. I could not endure another day like this one. These four angels deserved a strong Mumma, a Mumma in control, not this broken shell of a Mumma.

Time passed by in a blur after this. I held all four babies, I knew it was going to be a while before I saw them again.

I stepped into the ambulance, watched my house disappear as we silently drove towards the hospital. A sense of relief washed over me. Maybe now I would get the help I had needed for so long. I was admitted onto the ward, shown my room. I had to answer what seemed like endless questions, I was spent, I just wanted to sleep. I was eventually given some medication and fell into a fitful, nightmare filled sleep. I awoke the next morning to a strange new reality.

The Nut House.

# In patient

It was a mixed ward. Each patient with their own bedroom complete with shower and toilet. There was a dining room, a mixed tv room, an outside space, an art room and seperate male and female tv rooms.

It was a daunting place to be. It was filled with a fair few people of all ages at varying stages of their own mental battles. Some were obviously in a far worse state than others, hallucinating and quite glaringly ill, others seemed just like any one from the street, normal.

I tried to keep to myself, I wasn't interested in making friends, I just wanted to get better so that I could get home to my babies.

The first day I met with the psychiatrist, he fired a lot of questions at me before agreeing that a stay on the ward would be beneficial.

That evening at visiting time HE visited. HE sat at a dining table with me for around two minutes then said HE was going for a cigarette. So I sat and waited, watching the other family members, hugging their loved ones, chatting. It was nice. Then HE returned, I felt awkward, I was adjusting to the new medications. I focused my attention on a bottle of pop that I had on the table, I pushed it around in circles. Once I had asked about my babies, I had nothing to talk to HIM about. HE told me I was being weird, I laughed, asked HIM if HE realised where I was. HE then told me that his mother had offered to come down and help him with the children. Something I had been begging HIM to ask for months. If HE had have asked, I could have still been at home. I pointed this out, was shouted at, then HE left.

I stayed in my room until supper.


The following days merged into a seamless blur.

Some nights the fire alarm would sound as one of the residents had difficulty sleeping and acted out of a night time. There was often shouting. Every ten minutes or so a light would shine through the door as the nurses performed their routine checks.

Finally after a few days, the children were allowed to visit. I was escorted to a side room outside of the ward, a nurse sat just outside. Inside the room were my babies, my Dad and HIM. I gave my babies as many cuddles as I could. My little Mumma's boy refused hugs. He seemed angry with me. The girls chattered on about their week. Baby boy ran around as he normally did, filled with energy. I played a game with the girls. I asked HIM to stop baby boy destroying things, he was just a boisterous toddler but he did need to be kept an eye on. It all got a little much and I began to cry. All I wanted was to be ok and be back with my babies, but even this half an hour visit had proved too much. Again I was shouted at. The visit was over, I headed back to my room and sobbed.

The magic cure I was so hoping for hadn't arrived. The medication was working in that it calmed me somewhat. But I was still being shouted at every day down the phone. I watched other people at visiting time. These people had love, their visitors actually cared about their wellbeing. The hugs were genuine.

My visitor, each time HE would visit, the man that had vowed to love, protect and be there for me, in sickness and health, each time HE was there, visiting me in hospital, at the lowest point in my life so far, HE would reprimand me for being selfish then whinge to me how hard his life was. That wasn't love. I know I didn't feel love for HIM, but what HE had for me can't have been love either.

I was an inpatient on a psychiatric ward, seperated from the four little people that gave my life meaning. I knew at that point that I deserved more. That they deserved more. I knew that whilst I was shackled to HIM, whilst HIS feelings were considered more important, that I was never going to heal. If in that moment that made me selfish, so be it. I ended the marriage.

What that would mean moving forward I had no idea. I was twenty seven years old, had spent the last nine years beholden to a man that simply wanted to control me, destroying any thought of personal progression I had ever attempted. I couldn't get much lower than where I currently lay could I?

So that was that. Marriage over!

My time on the ward continued. I have many stories from that time, but they are not mine to tell and also not my focus here.

After four weeks, I needed to get out. Certain people on the ward were scaring me. I needed a safe haven, I didn't feel I could get that there. I enquired about leaving. As long as I continued with the treatment as an outpatient and had an address to go to, I was permitted to leave.

A bedsit was found and in I moved.

A cold empty room, white walls, wooden floor. I had a sofa bed and a TV, that was it. There was a small kitchen, a bathroom and a closet for storage. My new home. It was empty, it was quiet, I missed my babies terribly.

I was permitted to visit them for two hours, twice per week. HE had to supervise.

I could understand why, but that didn't lessen the pain.

All I had ever wanted was to be the best Mumma and I had failed catastrophically. They were left with a man that had never even bothered with them. I had to get better, I had to fix myself, I had to get back to being Mumma, so they at least stood some chance of a happy childhood.

I registered with a new GP as the bedsit was in a town 10 miles outside the village where the children were. She was honestly the best GP I had ever had. She seemed to genuinely care. When I explained to her how I had found the art room in the hospital quite cathartic, she tried to find art therapy classes for me to attend. She gave me a list of options for various different groups.

I began to attend a Bipolar support group. It was interesting to hear the experiences of others with the diagnosis. My own episodes seemed to differ in their longevity. The symptoms sounded the same but mine seemed to come and go far more rapidly.

I arranged to meet up with one of the ladies for coffee. It was nice to have another human to speak with.

I was lost.

I had been so busy for so many years. Babies, Nanny, more babies. I really couldn't adapt to this new normal. I hated it.

Seven months I stayed in that bedsit. During that time HE kept creating problems, making things difficult. Began to use the children as weapons. If I wasn't reacting how HE wanted or disagreed on something HE would threaten to take away my visiting hours. Bear in mind I wasn't better, I was still quite poorly, vulnerable. I very much needed support, which was distinctly absent. I remember after one argument, I had told HIM I had been meeting this lady for coffee. HE was furious. Group was for support, not to make friends, why was I making friends with crazy people, did I not want to get better?

I do wonder if HE realised what support is and how we women get it.

I was instructed never to meet her again or I would never see the children again.

I was so broken. I was just trying to rebuild some semblance of a life. If I didn't have my babies, I didn't have anything. I was hurting so much inside.

Perhaps HE was right, I was pathetic, useless. Maybe they would be better off without me altogether. Nobody wanted me, nobody liked me, I was completely alone.

I cut myself that day.

It wasn't an attempt to end my life, it was an attempt to refocus the pain. I just could not cope with how deep and searing the internal aching was. I broke a razor and used a single blade to slash at my arm.

It bled quite badly, but my emotions were numbed, I felt peaceful.

I phoned the crisis team for the second time that day, they called an ambulance and I was taken to hospital to be patched up. They gave me some painkillers and called one of their psyche team to come and see me. My anti psychotic dose was increased.

Apparently whilst I was being seen to HE had tried calling me, when I hadn't answered HE had driven to my flat, peering through my window HE had seen the blood on the floor and somehow HE had tracked me down. HE appeared at the hospital. Literally the last person I wanted to see. But drugged up and crying I was taken back to the house. I slept on the sofa, my babies snuggled in. That was all I wanted forever. My beautiful babies snuggled in close.

## Bye Babies

Some time after this HE decided that the house was to be sold and HE was taking the children to Newcastle. I didn't understand why, but HIS mind was made up.

But then it became urgent, HE couldn't wait, so HE sold the house for half it's value to a buy now for cash company. I don't ever remember signing anything, so I'm not sure if my signature was forged somehow. It was only half HIS to sell. It was a mistake to have agreed to include HIS name on the deed in the first place. Anyway, here we were, HE had sold it from under me without my consent and scurried away with my children to stay at HIS mothers.

My own mother had recently moved from Spain to Wales and so I moved out of the bedsit and in with her.

My angels meanwhile, hundreds of miles away, sharing a bunk bed in a box room in a place where playing and giggling found you chastised.

What was this life? What on earth had happened to make this a reality?

Daily life was now rather empty. A spare part at my Mum's, I felt so out of place, disconnected.

I would pop into the local pub with my stepdad for an hour or so everyday before Mum finished work. It was refreshing to partake in human interaction. I was quite muted really, due to the medication. But a glimmer of the real person that I was peeked out. It was just buried underneath a massive sense of loss and displacement.

I shouldn't be here twiddling my thumbs or engrossing myself in boxsets. I should be playing with my little boys, building towers, knocking them down, laughing, running round in the park. Or plaiting my girlies hairs, singing songs, tickling and giggling. I should be a Mumma.

Baby boy's third birthday was approaching, I had purchased his gifts, bought the other three a few little bits I knew they would love. HIS auntie had said I could stay at hers, so I was finally able to go and visit with my beautiful little angels. I drove up, I saw them.

It was such a strange experience. They were my babies. I was the one that had always been there for them, done everything for them.

Now, I was being watched like a hawk. I couldn't be alone with them, felt like I was being scrutinised constantly.

I visited with them at their Nana's flat. My heart ached to see how they were now living. Cramped into a tiny box room, without their toys and possessions. They had lost their Mum, their home and this was their existence. Sure they had their favourite cuddlies and a few bits, but they had no space to play. I remember we were messing on in the living room, their Nana was in the yard smoking, she shouted at us to be quiet. They were just laughing, excited to see their Mumma and thinking in that moment they were free to have fun as they would normally have done so with me. Wrong!

I held so much guilt. It was my fault they were here.

I needed to get myself moved so I could see them more. This was not a situation that should continue. Yet, I was helpless.

Each time we were together it was in someone else's house or garden, it felt as though those others had more say with the children I had grown in my body and raised to that point. I was an outsider in my children's lives. All because I was sick and nobody had helped me. It should have been HIM that had disappeared from their lives, they probably wouldn't have noticed. But bitterness and blame fixes nothing.

I had to bite my tongue when others that didn't know my children reprimanded them. I had to adjust to being a spectator in the lives of those I had created. It tore me apart.

I knew how they ticked, knew their strengths, their weaknesses, I knew the reasons behind the behaviour when they acted out, what it was they needed to be ok again. But I was forced to stand idly by whilst other people told me how things were.

I made certain that the times I did get with my angels was fun. That cuddles were fairly distributed and that Mumma was smiling throughout.

I would grit my teeth when I saw HIM acting as though HE were the perfect parent, as though HE had always been active with them and that their interests were at the heart of all HE did.

Each and every time I left, it felt fresh. I was leaving my heart behind. I would drive back to Wales and then sleep for two days. Grieving all over again. Grieving for the life I had lost, the time I was losing, for the control I lacked. The kicker really, was that I had never been a bad parent. They were always at the forefront of my mind. It wasn't my fault that I became ill. My mind messed up. I had truly only ever wanted the very best for them.

I knew they were hurting also. Short term, there was nothing I could do. I had no power, the only strength I possessed was being ok for their sakes.

It took four long months before I was able to move nearer.

Four months of fleeting visits, forging friendships with HIS family so that I could see them in a home environment.

Four months of empty days, looking forward to the weekend evenings in which I could go get blind drunk with the few acquaintances I had made. Two days per week where I could feel like a semi accepted human.

I began to see myself as more than a fuck up. Thought perhaps I did have it in me to make a full recovery. To have my children back with me.

HE still made it as difficult as HE could. Asked me to stop calling them so much as it disturbed them. Then some days I was visiting HE would decide I couldn't see them as planned. One evening I was there it was HIS cousin's birthday, she invited me out for a drink with her and a couple other family members. It was a night before I was due to see the children, so it made no difference to any plans. HE screamed down the phone at me, said I couldn't see the children as clearly I had only travelled up there to go get drunk. I failed to see HIS logic. HE was punishing them as much as me.

Another time when I was in Wales, I had arranged to visit with some friends that I had known in Spain, a small reunion. Myself and a friend would travel independently to stay with my former flatmate. Have a few drinks, reminisce. I had told big girl on the phone of my plans, she had met one of the friends a few times before, she liked to hear if Mumma was happy.


HE had found out, rang me some nine times whilst I was driving. I don't answer my phone when driving, ever. So I looked at my phone at the services when I'd pulled in for the loo at Somerset. I saw the missed calls and rang back, thinking a child was hurt. No, just HIS ego. Despite the fact we had been separated since October, ten months beforehand, HE still demanded complete control. Asked where I was and what I was doing. When I told HIM, HE went ballistic. Told me that if I didn't turn around and go home, that I would never see the kids again. Said he would lie to social services, go to court and make sure I was permanently banned from ever going near them .

What else could I do, faced with that.

In hindsight, I should have lied. But honesty is always my default. So I turned around and drove back to my Mum's. Both friends were absolutely furious with me. They couldn't understand. They thought I had just changed my mind about going. That was another blow.

One of the friends, the one Big girl knew, she had been to visit me in the hospital twice. She was a good friend. We had visited each other in the UK a few times since moving back. Unfortunately she didn't understand the level of HIS manipulation. We had a huge row, which ended up with us not being friends for a while.

HE was still managing to isolate me from my friends. HE was laughing. HE had my children with HIS family whilst off galivanting. Here I was hundreds of miles away. Alone. My Mum tried to be supportive. But what could she feasibly do. I just wanted to be back with my babies.

Eventually though, October, I moved. I found a flat in the same town.

They moved into a brand new housing association house, I moved into a privately rented flat.

A new chapter was beginning.

# Part Four

Another New Life?

# Home sweet Home

I created a beautiful space for the kiddies, filled it with toys and decorated with bits I knew they would love. The flat had two bedrooms, a very large one at the front, it was a converted Edwardian house with high ceilings, the front bedroom would have once been a sitting room, I gave the children this room so as they had space to play and be free, I took the smaller room at the back. They absolutely adored their new room and were so happy to be able to stay at Mumma's. I had chosen a place just around the corner from their new school. So on the days that I had them through the week, we walked to school.

On those days my heart was filled. I felt like a proper Mumma again. Making meals, ironing uniforms, reading stories, playing. All the things I had missed so much.

I had them three days out of the seven. The rest of the time I was lost.

I tried to keep busy, would visit with HIS family. They were being really helpful, I almost felt accepted. There was an underlying doubt, a niggle that they were simply keeping an eye on me for HIM. But I had to try and drown that out.

Another issue that was causing a problem was that seemingly HE had a girlfriend that was around all the time. The children would moan about this girl and how they were forced to share their rooms with her two children. They would complain about how horrible her children were, how they would bite and swear. I asked HIM about this. We had agreed that should either of us move on, the children wouldn't be introduced to this person for a good few months. This girl had been around since they had moved up. Big girl had come to me very upset that she had heard HIM on the phone saying I love you quite soon after they had first moved into HIS mothers.

It wouldn't have been a problem, but HE lied about it. Said that they were just friends. But since they had moved into their new house the girlfriend and her children were around more often than not.

One evening I was at HIS cousins, we were just hanging out, planning on getting a chippy for tea and watching a film. I received a very panicked phone call. I rushed around to the children's house, HE came to the car. Big girl was very upset, HE got his side in first then brought her over to the car. I asked HIM to leave us alone as Big girl was sobbing and it was clear she didn't want HIM around right then. Reluctantly HE left, but HE stayed by HIs front door, watching.

I climbed into the back of the car and sat her on my lap, tried to calm her down.

She hated HIM. HE was a liar. Why couldn't they live with me, HE was horrible.

Apparently she had needed HIS help, they were supposed to be watching a DVD, but the player had glitched, so she went to get Daddy to fix it. She had knocked on the door but received no answer, so she opened the door. She caught HIM and the "friend" in a compromising position. HE screamed at her, told her to get out, how dare she walk into HIS bedroom, they should be watching the DVD.

Obviously this nine year old girl having had her suspicions confirmed immediately lost her cool.

The tale HE had spun was that they were fully clothed and hugging as friend had been upset, Big girl simply had the wrong end of the stick.

This sobbing child I held in my arms was adamant that they were unclothed and kissing. I calmed her as best as I could. She begged to come with me, HE wouldn't allow it as it wasn't my day.  So I had to leave her there.  To be lied to again.  To be told that what she had seen with her own eyes wasn't true.

I couldn't have cared any less that HE had moved on, what bothered me was that those precious children, who had already been through so much, had to face new realities before having the time to settle.  Their protection, care and emotions should be priority.  HE had days child free, in those days, HE could do as HE pleased.  It didn't need to be in their consciousness, let alone laid out right in front of them.

Fact was, they wanted Mumma.

HE hadn't been around, then all of a sudden HE's the only one there.  HE didn't really want them.  When they had first moved up the children had been left with HIS mother every evening while HE entertained HIMSELF elsewhere.

I was told of one evening when HIS mother had plans herself, so asked HIM to make sure HE was back to sit with HIS children, HE hit the roof.  Screamed , shouted, broke things then took the kids and stayed in a hotel for the night.

The children also told me that when I would leave after visiting, they would cry.  They didn't want me to leave, they wanted to come with me.  HE would shout at them for crying!  Who does that?

I felt so powerless.  I was powerless.  My children needed to be with me, the person that actually cared about their wellbeing.  There's more to parenting than simply putting a roof over their heads and food in their bellies.

I was feeling so much better in myself.  I felt ready to be a proper Mumma again.  So I asked for more days.  Denied.

Imaginary problems were created, I was prevented from seeing them at all.

Even a completely sane, rational person would react emotionally when told they can't see their children. But any reaction other than complete compliance was proof of my instability, further proving to HIM that I was unable to care for the children.

Was this a cycle that would repeat forever? Lost again and left to wonder why.

I had genuinely never been anything but a doting Mumma. Their needs always above my own. It was now over a year since my hospitalisation. The feeling of having forgotten something when I left home persisted. Had I left the oven on? Forgotten my purse? The reality was, it was my babies I didn't have, a part of me was missing. I floated about life without them like a ghost. It was a half life, a mere existence. They were my focus, my reason for living. I didn't matter, but they did.

Everywhere I went I was reminded of what I didn't have. If I was at HIS family's, I would be with HIS cousin's children, just a spare part watching another person interact with their children, making me ache for mine.

Walking around shops, mothers with their children, exhausted fed up mothers, shouting at their toddlers. It hurt. It felt like a winded sensation, I couldn't catch my breath, my eyes would begin to tear up and in that moment I vehemently hated that mother.

Shouting at her precious angel for just being a child. Why did she get to have her child, she didn't even care that the poor mite was now sobbing. She didn't deserve to be a mum.

Of course you can never tell a person's circumstances by observing a fraction of their day in a public place. I just missed my own children so much, every minute not with them was painful. Especially when I knew that it was out of spite. They missed me, they were miserable, but I couldn't have them with me.

The festive season approached. I was permitted to have them from three pm on Christmas day, overnight until boxing day evening.

Christmas morning, I woke up and cried.

I should have been awoken by excited chattering as the four of them attempted to be as quiet as they could, opening the stockings that Santa had left at the end of their beds. I should have lain there smiling as the pitter patter of hurried little feet made their way into my room. Listening to their excited squeals and watching their delighted faces as they tore wrapping paper from each gift.

Instead, I woke to silence. Alone.

Happy Christmas, pinged a text.

It wasn't happy, it was far from it. It was miserable. I wanted to fall asleep, to wake up and find it had all been a terrible nightmare.

I pulled myself out of bed, washed , dressed and headed over to HIS cousin's. I played with their children, pushing down my misery to focus on making those kiddies smile.

I had been invited to stay for Christmas Lunch. HIS Auntie had bought me some gifts. It was so unexpected, caught me off guard, I shed a happy tear.

My dinner was plated up for me and I took it home with me as they would have sat down to eat at the time I was collecting my babies.

I set off and collected them. I heard all about their morning, what Santa had bought them, they were high from the festive buzz of it all. This is what it was all about. These four little people.

We arrived at my flat and they saw the pile of presents beneath the tree. They dived in.

I sat on the sofa soaking it all in, their excited shrieks, flying paper, the shouted thank yous and the squishy, sticky hugs. It was finally Christmas.

These were the moments I lived for. There really was nothing else.

The New year rolled in, pointless resolutions filled everybody's thoughts.

I planned a trip to Luton, I can't remember the reason.

Visiting my Mummy friends hammered home how utterly broken my life was. I held their babies, the ones I had missed the births of, chatted with my friends and realised that minus my children, which I now was, I had very little in common with them anymore.

I felt all the more alone.

I spent time with various people, including my sisters. It heightened my sense of not belonging. I was displaced, a stranger in my own life. I belonged nowhere. Growing steadily more despondent.

A few weeks after returning home I travelled back down again. My friend from Spain, the one that had visited me in hospital, her Mother had been ill for sometime and had passed away. I went to try and be some form of support at the funeral. I spent a few days with my friend, she had been close with her Mum and was obviously deeply upset. I tried to be as supportive as I could. It brought up my own grief, from losing my Nan. How I missed her. How very different my life had become. I felt a sense of deep shame. How could she be proud of me now? What did I have? What had I achieved?

I had allowed a man, my husband, to destroy everything.

HE stole from her, yet there HE was in HIS shiny new house, with my babies. Whilst I sat in a drafty flat weeping for all I had lost.

Nothing was mine anymore but a desperately fractured reality.

Time ticked by. Some weeks half filled with Mumma duties. Some not.

The weeks that we were punished because HE deemed something I had done as a punishable offense, seemed to last an eternity.

## Stepping stones

I started dating, an attempt to feel human.

To have something for myself. It killed a few hours in the evenings I was alone.

I felt odd. It was difficult to explain my situation. Mothers have their children, if a mother doesn't, usually there's addiction issues or something.

How much information would cut it? That I didn't have custody, but it wasn't my fault.

I saw a man for around three months. It was nothing particularly serious. We would go out for meals, watch movies. Conversation was kept quite shallow. I didn't let much out.

I think I was probably still scared of my own emotions and I couldn't risk letting them out, possibly losing control. This was just an easy distraction from that. A few hours a couple of days per week.


I moved into a council flat, three bedrooms, more security, more of a home for the children.

Things ended with the guy I had been seeing around the same time that I moved. I was pretty apathetic about it.

I set about creating a proper home for my babies. We shared some happy times there.

Big Girl had a sleepover for her Birthday, she wouldn't have been allowed or have wanted one at HIS, so it was nice that she could do that.

There were always toys out, endless giggles. They were free to be children.

It inspired me to try and gain custody. I sought a solicitor, started the correct procedures. Unfortunately it backfired. HE refused to attend Mediation, which was a necessary step, HE also lied to the solicitor.

He removed contact, again.

I was devastated, again.

Goodness knows how this was all affecting the impressionable young minds at the centre of this chaos. I had been so hopeful, hopes dashed. As a result my medication was increased.

In another attempt to find some normal, I started dating again.

I began seeing someone that was very keen to keep me around, asked me to attend an event with him some three months away.

It felt nice to be wanted. So we became a couple.

I met his family and I fell in love with them. I felt a part of something. As though I had a place. Still a little on the outside, but it was far better than where I had been.

From the very beginning it was clear that C was the boss. I was told how to behave and what was expected of me. I went along with it.

In my limited experience, that's how it worked. The male was in control.

My overall memories of this time are quite clouded. I almost floated through days.

I don't remember much of 2012 at all really. Medication clearly too high.

I started a hairdressing course in the September. Thought I may have been able to make friends as well as create some kind of future. I found it very difficult to bond with anyone, I hated having to explain why I didn't have my kids. I mostly just listened to the other women interact whilst trying to learn as much as I could.

I remember on one day having to rush to the toilets and sobbing in a cubicle. C had taken issue with something and had basically decided not to be with me anymore. Someone had heard me crying and I was taken to the college counsellor. Had to tell her my story from scratch.

She said I seemed detached from what I told her. Of course I was. I had told this story so many times yet, to those I spoke it, it was just a sad story.

To me, it was my shattered subsistence. I hated the pity in people's faces. I didn't want or need their sympathy, so I spoke it as though I were just telling a story. Just words and happenings, no emotion. I didn't want to feel it. The pain was still too strong. It was debilitating. If I allowed myself to truly feel, I would drown.

# Looking up

Christmas came around again. That year I woke up at C's, opened gifts from him. I felt so much happier than I had the previous year.

It was arranged that I would collect the children after dropping C at his parents house.

C asked me to stay for gift giving at his parents. It was plenty of notice, so I called HIM , said I would be a half an hour later than planned to collect the children as C's parents had a gift for me.

HE kicked off! I was being selfish. I was putting myself first as usual, so forget it, spend the day with C. I tried to reason with him. It was only thirty minutes. HE just shouted some more. I couldn't have the children. I had ruined Christmas.

I drove to C's parents in tears, we exchanged gifts, they invited me to stay for dinner, I thanked them and settled into watching a movie. C was pottering around with his brother.

Then I got a call, pick the kids up within ten minutes or never see them again.

I thanked the family for the invitation, explained I had to go and raced around the corner to collect the children. We went back to my flat and made the most of our time together.

We had a great time. We always did.


At around six am on boxing day I heard a noise. I assumed it was Big boy as he always woke up early, I snuggled down into the covers, smiling to myself, knowing that my babies were safe, happy and nearby.

A heavy hand hit my face. That was no child. My eyes shot open as the hand again hit my face, accompanied by the words, "You stupid bitch" repeated as the hand fell again and again. I sat up confused. It was C. I had left my front door unlocked, so to teach me the error of my ways he had just walked in quietly and decided to slap and chastise me.

I tried to downplay as best as I could. The children were here, he was still drunk and hadn't yet slept. So I got up and entertained the children whilst he got into my bed and slept the day away.

2013 rolled in, kiddies were at mine as New Years had always been our little party night. It started when the girls were tiny and I was left at home with them, I would wake them up just before midnight to watch fireworks.

We danced, we sang, we ate. We brought that New Year in with smiles and laughter, one happy Mumma and her four little nutters. I wished every day could be like this.

It turned out to be a tumultuous year. Access was continually taken away due to whims. Ridiculous things such as daring to voice an opinion on something the children were doing. I mean, what did I know, I was only their part time Mumma.

The introduction of the bedroom tax was near, it wasn't in actuality a tax, it was a reduction in benefit payments for those in receipt of housing benefit. So as my children didn't live with me, it meant I could no longer have a bedroom for them. My housing benefit would be cut by 25% for the two bedrooms I apparently didn't need. This threw me. It meant I couldn't afford to stay in the flat. I started looking for work.

A guy C knew said about vacancies where he worked, so I applied. I got a job there and left college.

It meant that I could stay in the flat, also as I could choose my own shifts, it meant I could make sure to be free at the times I was scheduled to have the children.

There was no wriggle room on that. Even if it were down to working hours, HE wouldn't allow any days to change, ever. If I did need to ask, due to appointments with Dr's or interviews, I was being selfish, didn't care about the kids, didn't deserve them.

It was March and that meant my 30th birthday.

My best friend, (the one from Spain) was coming up with her new boyfriend. I hadn't yet met him and she hadn't met C. She had booked a hotel room in the same place as her, for C and I as a gift.

It was all set to be a wonderful reunion and a joyous celebration.

I got ready at the hotel with my friend, we then went to C's for pre drinks before heading into town to a fancy bar that C bounced at.

As to be expected with C and his mates, pre drinks meant getting absolutely wasted on booze along with copious amounts of cocaine.

Celebrating with me were my friend and her boyfriend, C and two of his mates. I was so happy that my best friend was here.

We arrived at the bar, my head already spinning from the booze, it was a beautiful venue, we were ushered upstairs into a private area. C had booked the VIP section, I had no idea, that had been a nice surprise.

We ordered drinks and I sat myself next to my best friend so that we could catch up properly. It was so lovely to have her here. Especially as we had been friends since we were around seventeen. We chatted away, oblivious to the world around us.

I was suddenly aware of fingers clicking in my face. I looked up and C was angry with me. He made me move to a seat beside him just as a cake was brought out and everyone began to sing. I was so embarrassed. A lovely thought yes, but I hated that much attention, kind of wanted the world to swallow me up, it seemed as though the whole bar was singing. I blew out the candles, said my thank-you's and we continued drinking.

We moved onto a club.

C had pretty much vanished, I was chatting with his two friends, trying to encourage the single one to find a girl. I was pointing out options and generally just having a giggle.

More drinks were imbibed. Dancing, laughs, high jinx and merriment. The rest of the night passed by in a blur of drunkenness.

Back in the hotel room, C was furious. I had ignored him all night. I was a slag. I was sat next to his mate in the first bar because I obviously wanted him, then I'd been flirting with him in the club, why hadn't I danced with C.

Obviously his perception had been very different to mine.

This now escalated into shouting, threatening, smashing things.

This was my thirtieth birthday. A night you're supposed to remember forever and it had morphed into an absolute nightmare. I remember smashing a bottle and attempting to cut myself with it, I just wanted the night to end.

C left, went home and I cried myself to sleep, alone in my birthday gifted hotel room, my life once again flipped upside down.

That was the end of the relationship.

## A Victim

I continued working, saw the kids maybe once a week, the rest of the time I cried.

I longed for a friend, somebody to tell me I would be ok.

C was still texting me, which was confusing. If I had had my babies, I really wouldn't care as much.

I was thirty years old and had spectacularly failed at adult life.

C kept visiting every week or so. He came to my flat more since we had split up than the entire time we spent together.

During this time I began training in a call centre. It was all very new and exciting, I was desperately trying to create a new me.

One of the times C had come around, he punched me, rib-shot, he called it.

He had said he was only messing on and hadn't meant to hurt me, but he had.

He had broken my ribs, it hurt to breathe for weeks. People at work asked what had happened, I told the truth.

A month or so later C decided that we should be together again. I agreed. I was happy again. But, it was different.


C told me to book a restaurant for a nice meal, so I asked around at work for recommendations, I chose one and booked a table. It was a really nice place, sophisticated, upmarket. Not the kind of establishment I was used to. The whole night I was on edge.

C was behaving really oddly. Kept complaining that his foot hurt and was constantly bending down to rub it. I was embarrassed.

Once our main courses had been eaten, he asked for our plates to be cleared, which I thought was rather rude. Then he was whingeing about his foot again, he bent down, I was preparing for the embarrassment of him removing his shoe.

Instead, he was now on one knee with a ring in his hand asking me to marry him.

The whole restaurant were staring, everything was spinning in slow motion. I said yes and the whole area erupted into applause. I was more in shock than anything else.

We received a complimentary bottle of champagne from the staff. We took it outside to sit on the terrace, although he moaned that he didn't like it and got a free bottle of cider for himself. We phoned our parents from the terrace. Nobody seemed very pleased.

C's mum asked about having kids as she knew I had been sterilised. My mum asked where we were going to live. Never mind all that. We were engaged. I had a fiancé.

I had never been engaged before, only married. This was new, it felt nice. A warm happy buzz rippled through me.


The happy didn't last too long though.

Three days after our engagement would be the first time that he raped me.

Suddenly the ring on my finger became a symbol of his ownership, I was his property. I must obey, or face the consequences.

It became significantly worse.

I was drugged in order to answer questions that were fired at me or drugged into a submissive state so that he could abuse my body without my protesting or crying out in pain.

His drug taking became more and more a daily occurrence.

We moved in together, a new council flat, around the corner from his old place so that it was still convenient for his work. Around the time we moved in, he was fired from his job due to his drug abuse.

I was now a full time punch bag. I was hit, spanked, my hair was pulled. Kidney punches, together with dead arms or legs were his favourite. If I had been particularly naughty he would bend me over his knee, pull down my pants and stick his fingers into my back passage, whilst laughing hysterically at my distress.

Life was horrendous.

We went away for a week, I was planning on finishing things when we returned home. Whilst we were away we received the news that his Dad was diagnosed with cancer. Stage 4 mesothelioma .

I couldn't leave him now. So I stayed.

By now, C was a full blown benzo addict. Not content with himself being out of it , he would continually find ways to spike me. Sometimes I caught it before it was too late other times, he was sneakier. After one such spiking, I ended up being hospitalised. I had attended a Dr's appointment and passed out in the surgery, an ambulance was called and I was taken to hospital. They didn't believe my story, thought I had taken the drugs myself, intentionally. Social services were informed and I was back to supervised visits with the children.

Life was meant to have improved, but it had become so much worse than it had ever been. This must have been my punishment for letting the children down in the first place. I must have deserved it.

Daily life was like navigating a minefield, one perceived slight, smack.

I accepted it. My penance.

Fast forward to October 2014.

Make or break, do or die.

The day that I sat crying after another beating, took a knife and cut my wrist vertically in an attempt to end the constant suffering that had become my life.

The clarity I felt once I saw the blood begin to spill was instant.

It was my duty to stay alive. I had four little angels that needed me. I had to continue fighting, for them. I couldn't leave them behind.

I wrapped the wound and phoned an ambulance.

The police were sent to sit with me until an ambulance was available. I sat curled up with a compress on the wound, shivering underneath a blanket and staring into space.

C was home, he was in bed. The police told him what I had done, informed him I would be taken to hospital, he stayed in bed.

I was stitched up at hospital, spoke with a lovely lady with the crisis team and eventually in the morning of the next day, I was taken home.

C had gone to work, I had the flat to myself. So I showered and slept.

At three pm C text me asking if I was ok. I told him no, I wasn't.

When he came home I told him we were over. A few days later due to him dragging his heels, I found him somewhere else to live and he left.

Again he tried to weasel his way back, but I was determined.

In the early hours of one morning, he knocked on the door. I had already had the locks changed as I didn't trust him. Somehow though he had gained entry into the building and was standing knocking on my front door. I sleepily opened the door and he pushed his way in.

He raped me again. Only this time, It felt different as we weren't together. The other times, as messed up as it seems, I had justified it to myself, he was my fiancé. But this time, he had forced his way into my home and violently taken what he wanted from me whilst I kicked and screamed. Afterwards he walked around the flat as though nothing had happened. Just sat on my sofa casually rolling himself a joint.

Eventually he left and I went back to bed.

I was so broken, so alone. I tried reaching out, thinking someone would care enough to come and visit, show me some kindness. Nobody did.

Fortunately, my best friend was already booked to come and stay for a few days, so I waited for her then confided in her the realities of what had happened.

We had a great visit. We built my bed, as since moving in C and I had just slept on a mattress on the floor. We put up some curtains in the bedroom. Made the place look nice, girly, trying to eradicate C's presence.

When she left, I made an appointment with a rape counsellor.

It was only during my talk with her that the true extent of the abuse and control became apparent to me.

Absurd as it seems having read some of the terrible times I endured, together with all the parts I've left out. In my vulnerability, my medicated, lonely state, I clung to the good times and accepted the terrible as my punishment.

I truly felt I deserved it.

I was a pathetic person, weak. I had failed to be a good wife. Failed as a mother. I was just completely useless. There was nothing that I could do right.

## Time to Heal

I began to read a lot. Ways to cope with the past traumas. Tactics for change.

I would spend hours online reading scholarly articles on psychology.

Gaining insight on why those in my life that had hurt me behaved in such a way and why it was I had been susceptible to their abuse. I spent nine months alone, healing. I learned how to be strong. How to be in control of myself and my emotions.

I managed to get access to the children more regularly as well. Which was great.

I started seeing a guy that hailed from my hometown. Which when living four hundred miles away from the place, was pretty odd. We had even unbeknown to us at the time, lived in the same street at opposite ends.

We spent a lot of time talking about life's deeper intricacies. It was as though we were meant to meet. Not for keeps. Just as a tool for deeper understanding, learning lessons together. It lasted three months. But what I took from that short time was invaluable, I now had a much broader knowledge of myself, of who I truly was, what I wanted out of life and relationships. He also introduced me to meditation, which I now use daily. So although to those outside of it, two dysfunctional people coming together for a brief moment in time may have seemed like nothing, I really do feel it was instrumental in the path I am on in this journey of life. I only hope he managed to take as much forwards from the relationship as I did.

What followed were the greatest changes. I continued reading, never considering falling back into the bad habits and coping mechanisms I had relied upon previously. I think, I was finally fixed.

By far the best part of all this positive change was that, in the September of 2015, Baby girl came to live with me.

HE said that HE was unable to cope with her challenging behaviour. That challenging behaviour had simply been her standing up for herself, but it worked out great for she and I.

I made the second bedroom more focused on being just her room, rather than the four of theirs. She was very pleased with the alterations and settled in. She was a much happier girl and I was now a much happier Mumma.

Big Boy wanted to move in as well, but I knew HE wouldn't allow it. I asked anyway. Denied.

In fact I was taken to court for a Child arrangements order to be drawn up.

By this time I had actually made a local friend. She helped me with what I should ask for and attended court with me in support.

Visiting times and days were for the first time officially defined and Baby girl's main residence was with me.

This was a catalyst. If I could gain custody of one child, there was nothing to stop getting the other three, not really. I told Big boy that we could gradually move his belongings over to mine, try for extra days and eventually push HIM again.


Life settled into a new kind of normal.

Baby girl's behaviour at school improved, lines of communication between myself and the school were open, so working in unison we managed to get across to Baby girl exactly what was expected of her. The improvement in Baby girl pushed me further into the desire to be ok. We were now creating a life in which we wanted to exist.

The friend that I had made, I met via an online support group for people with my mental illness, which was now said to be Borderline Personality Disorder. She only had traits, not full blown. But in talking with her, seeing the life she had with a functioning family unit, it gave me hope. Maybe I wasn't a lost cause.

I knew that I had healed myself a lot, working on my reactions to events and finding healthy coping strategies.

My strength, my new found sense of self, it was all good and spurred me on.

My thirty third birthday was close and with it a crazy flash of an idea. I had received some money in lieu of gifts towards finishing a tattoo I had started. But what if I put that money to better use?

I rang HIM, told HIM my idea and surprisingly HE agreed.

I had seen a discount voucher online for a caravan holiday. I scoured the list to find one within my budget and booked it.

For the first time I was going to take my babies on holiday by myself.

Just myself and my four beautiful nutters for five whole days of fun.

Morecambe Bay here we come.

The holiday was booked for the end of May, so we had a few months to plan activities and build excitement.

# Part Five

Winds of change start blowing

## Glimmers of a smile

I had a hire car booked from the day before we were due to leave. Give me a chance to get used to it before making a long journey with four excited kiddos in the car.

I drove around for a few hours, was satisfied that I could manage. But now I had time to kill, a vehicle and nothing to do. I was sat in the car park of a pub, contemplating going inside. I had a scroll through my dating app, read a few profiles and paused on one that I found intriguing.

I liked to take the time to actually read them, as what I was looking for was a connection, a significant other. Someone to match my personality, to challenge me, without being a negative influence. Someone that I could walk side by side with through life, each bringing our own strengths and picking the other up in their weakness.

This guy, seemed to fit the bill. He had a certain allure that the 95% of posers on there lacked. Good looking, irreverent. I was just about to send him a message when my inbox flashed notifying me that he had sent me a message. Ha, spooky.

I opened the message and replied. We exchanged a few opening pleasantries then I hit on an idea. I had nothing to do, he had stated in his profile that he was spontaneous, so I asked if he fancied meeting up. We agreed on an hours time in a pub a short drive from where I was.

I arrived at the unfamiliar setting and head to the bar, I ordered myself a soft drink. As the barman went about making my beverage I was aware of a presence behind me, I turned, had a momentary face flush and a bit of a wobble. It was him, so much better looking in the flesh, wow.

We took our drinks and settled at a table in a quiet corner. The chatter was easy, we seemed to get on really well. I found myself captivated by his eyes. Bluey green pools of hidden depths, drawing me in. I wondered what secrets lay beneath. Hoped I would one day find out.

After a time, feeling hungry and not interested in the limited bar menu, we decided to take a drive. We went in his car and headed for the coast.

We took a leisurely stroll along the seafront casually getting to know one another, we ate chips on a bench watching the sea, fed a random dog that came to say hello. All in all it was a lovely first date. No hidden agendas, no misunderstandings, just two people enjoying one another's company. We agreed on a second meeting once I returned from my holiday.

# Holidaze

Finally, that longed for day arrived. I set off to collect my tribe and off we went on our first holiday. It took far too long to get there as I kept getting us lost, but eventually we arrived.

All of our belongings unloaded and in the caravan, we changed and head out to a restaurant for our evening meal. We ended the evening in the campsite entertainment venue, fizzy pop and dancing to cheesy songs.

They were so happy. Seeing the joy on each of their faces filled me with immeasurable bliss. This was going to be the best week.

We filled our days with fun activities, they knew I wasn't made of money and understood that fun needn't cost a lot.

We had taken some board games for inside the caravan. We swam at the campsite pool, had a trip to the cinema, discovered an amazing park which ate a whole day, had a couple meals out. We spent the evenings sampling the entertainment in the campsite bar and playing pool. I was enjoying the week as much as they seemed to be.

I noticed as the week drew on that they all seemed that little bit lighter. The threat of returning to HIM that usually weighed heavy upon them, was lifted. They were free and loving every second. Honestly was the best feeling, having them all. Waking up each morning to their excited chatter of the day ahead. It put an instant smile upon my face.

It unfortunately couldn't last forever and the week came to an end, we returned downcast and somewhat exhausted, back to reality.

We had however created some amazingly sweet memories, we also had that hope that some day we could do it all again.

A few days after we returned, G and I had that second date.

It was fantastic.

We got on so well, shared a similar humour and I just felt so comfortable in his presence. That first night we went to a rock bar in the city centre, had a raucous time. We crashed out on my living room floor stupidly inebriated. The next morning he went home for a shower and change of clothes and then came back, we went to McDonalds for a hang over breakfast, then drove around, went to a park for a walk.

The date didn't end, we were so enjoying our time together that we continued that night and into the next day. Day to day life and work came knocking so the heady dream that had been those first three days came to a close. But once I was child free again, we were back spending time together. After around three weeks we became an official couple.

Life was definitely looking up and going from strength to strength.


Of course HE would still make things as difficult as HE possibly could at times. Thing was though, HE no longer controlled me. I refused to take the bait. Believe me it was hard. Even after all the work I had done on myself, the fact that HE still took complete control of the children was infuriating.

Big boy began to stay extra nights at mine, essentially he was now at mine more than he was at HIS. We easily settled into this new way of being.

G and the children got on well. The children seemed to like him and could see how happy he was making Mumma. Which was encouraging.

There were now so many more happy days than there were stressful, revolving around HIM days. I still had to be careful what I said as the kick offs were never far from the surface.

# Levelling up

One day, I had called HIM to discuss something about one of the children. HE was not appreciative of my input. It was a Monday which meant that the previous evening Big Boy had stayed over at HIS and I would collect him from school that afternoon. That was the arrangement for the past six months.

Not today! I had apparently overstepped my power level, I was now forbidden to collect Big Boy, HE would collect him and keep him indefinitely. Big Boy was no longer permitted to live with me. The issue I phoned to discuss with HIM had been about one of the girls, this was just HIM exerting HIS perceived power.

I immediately telephoned the school, warned them that an issue was imminent and raced to the school as fast as the public transport I relied upon allowed. Fortunately HE had been banned from school premises some time ago, so I knew HE couldn't do anything until Big girl had finished school.

I met with the head and the pastoral lead, explained exactly what had happened. They were very familiar with the situation and HIS behaviour, having sat in on Social services meetings and obviously feeling the need to permanently bar HIM from the premises. They had a duty to inform the police, I agreed that it was sensible regardless of duty.

As I had suspected HE had sent Big girl in to collect Big boy. Big boy had been safely taken over to the afterschool club so he was witness to none of HIS ensuing hysterics. Unfortunately Baby boy and Big girl were. The Police got the history and an explanation of the days events plus child arrangements from myself and the school staff, they then head down to speak with HIM.

Whilst Police were speaking with HIM, the head and I watched from the window of her office, she told me that in the time Big boy had been predominately at mine, he had blossomed. For the first time in the five years he had been at that school, he had raised his hand to answer a question. He had been a member of that school since Reception year and had never before spoken up in class.

That had been nice to hear. My baby was comfortable.

The police decided that the best course of action would be to ask Big boy himself who he wished to go home with and that whosoever he picked was to be respected, the other parent must accept that. I agreed, HE agreed.

I requested that the pastoral Lead be present and explain it to him as I didn't want him to think he was in any kind of trouble, it would be quite scary for him for the police to suddenly be talking to him.

Big boy answered that he wished to come home with Mumma. HE was informed by the Police as the head ushered me around corridors to wait for Big boy. He appeared from a back way and gave me a big hug. We waited for the Police to come and give the all clear. They came over, told us that HE was leaving. I asked if they were absolutely sure as Big boy and I would be taking the metro home and HE may use that to his advantage, waiting near the station for a confrontation.

Very kindly the Police offered to drive us to the station.

We had won that battle. But he very fact that HE could still pull that rubbish, just wasn't on. It was fair to nobody.


A few days later I was expressing the frustration of HIS power trips to G. Explaining how much I wished I could just pick them up and take them away from HIM, let them be children and free of HIS ridiculous whims.

G asked why couldn't I.

As the conversation continued the realisation that maybe I could do that struck.

I spent hours telling other people that their lives were their own, that they needed to take responsibility for their own lives and happiness, yet here I was still beholden to a dictator, that really held no true authority over any of us anymore.

I was no longer under mental health teams, I kept my equilibrium through mindfulness and meditation. Two out of the four children were mostly resident with me, their behaviours and adjustments only improving under my support. So yeah, G was right.

Why couldn't I?

## Plotting

A plan began to develop.

I would go to Wales, somewhere near my Mum. But it needed to be kept very close to my chest. If HE so much as suspected anything, spanners would be thrown into the works.

I researched all the legalities, managed to get an appointment with a solicitor. It was feasible, I wouldn't be breaking any laws.

Of course HE could take me to court but unless HE could prove that I was medically or mentally unfit to care for them, there was nothing really HE could reasonably do.

G would join us when work commitments allowed.

I let Baby girl and Big boy in on the secret, as with them living with me, there would be times and conversations where I couldn't realistically hide it from them.

They were neither of them daft and we lived in a two bedroom flat, privacy was pretty much non existent.

As I had expected, they were thrilled, almost counted down the days.

My Mum was keeping an ear to the ground with regards to housing possibilities. I looked into an exchange as the flat was council, but unsurprisingly nobody with a three bed house in the picturesque region of Carmarthenshire wanted to swap their house for a two bedroomed flat in a high rise located in the east end of Newcastle.

In the June of 2017, I took a week long trip down to Wales to search myself for properties and to check out areas, schools etc.

The options were rather limited but this was something that needed to be done. It needn't be a perfect place, just somewhere that we could call home in order to escape.

As luck shone upon us, a three bedroom house with a garden and in a family centred area became available. It wasn't in the best condition, was a bit grotty truth be told. But beggars can't be choosers, it was big enough, close to good schools. I paid a deposit, signed a tenancy and decided on a starting date of July 14th, Baby boy's birthday.

Having been successful the previous year in taking them away on holiday, this time I basically told HIM. I was taking them away to Wales for two weeks at the start of the Summer holidays. Would be staying in a house of a friends of my Mum's. HE agreed. Children were told.

I popped into the boys school to speak with the head. I told her of the plan, told her Big boy was aware and very excited but that Baby boy was oblivious. She said that they would be truly missed but that she totally understood and thought I was absolutely doing the right thing and she was delighted for us. She also told me she was proud of me, strange thing to hear, she said I was a completely different person to the one that she first met six years ago. That meant a lot, I teared up a little.

Everything was falling into place. Loose ends were being tied. Schools were applied for down in Wales, it was all go.

G and I spent as much time together as possible, it would be quite some time before he could join us. That was going to a wrench. I soaked in as much as I could. Would find myself watching him sleep, just savouring every second. What we shared was so special, so different to anything that had come before. We had love, friendship and mutual respect. No games were played, we were up front and honest with each other with everything. I had finally found my perfect match, yet here I was actively moving away from him. The fact he was supportive of that decision and fully behind it, spoke wonders.

All of this was for the betterment of my children's lives. He understood that, which made me love him all the more.

Big Boy and Baby girl were growing increasingly amped up with excitement. There was a certain stop on the metro, that Big boy knew most of HIS family wouldn't be, as soon as we passed that station he would chatter away about the great escape.

Escaping the dictatorial control of their narcissistic father. We couldn't wait.

# Part Six

Wales: Take Two

## We are off

The day arrived.

The children had spent the night at HIS. I had told Big girl and Baby boy to pack as much as they could, we were going for two weeks after all and the welsh weather could be unpredictable.

My Dad and G were packing up the flat into a van and my Dad would follow down later that day. I was driving Dad's car.

The children piled their belongings into the boot, said their Goodbye's and off we set.

As we pulled out of HIS street Big boy turned around and loudly exclaimed,

"Good Riddance".

My sentiments exactly son, onwards to a new life filled with happiness.


We drove straight to my mum's as we had to collect the keys for Grandma's "friends" house. It was a week past the start of the tenancy as I had obviously needed to wait for schools to break for summer.

During that week my Mum and stepdad had been busy building children's beds and getting things ready for us. In the flat they had only had a triple bunk between the four of them, so now, with extra bedrooms and every day life together, they had their own beds.

We stopped over at Mum's as Dad had decided to stay over at G's and drive down the next day. It had been quite late when they had finished, so it made sense for him to make the long drive after a night's sleep.

So it was the following morning when I knew that Dad was en-route, that I broke the news to the two that were still in the dark as to the true nature of this trip.

We were all sat in Mum's front room and I explained that actually, this wasn't a holiday and the house we would be driving to later, was in fact ours and we lived here now.

The two reactions could honestly not have been any different.

Baby boy was super chill, just asked when he could get the rest of his stuff.

Big girl on the other hand took it badly.

She seemed terrified and furious in equal measure. She was adamant that I was breaking the law and would be arrested. I assured her that despite what she may have been told in the past by HIM, I had consulted a solicitor, made sure to read up on all legalities and that I was actually well within my legal rights. She was fearful of HIS reaction.

I asked her to trust me, that it had been a long time in planning and that it had been the only way I could see that would allow them to live with me without HIS interference.

The other three were ecstatic.

## Belonging

Fast forward to being settled in and mostly unpacked, now came the time that HE was told.

I have to admit my heart was racing as I dialled and waited for the call to connect.

I knew that we were safe, I was prepared for HIM to take me to court, I knew I wasn't strictly in the wrong, but still that fear had me. We had been under HIS rule for so long.

The call connected and I told HIM, very matter of fact. The children would not be returning, they lived with me now, here in Wales.

At first there was quiet disbelief, then HE must have thought on it and court was mentioned. I told HIM to go ahead.

The children were all happily playing out with their new found friends. Summer days spent the way that they should be, contented children making the most of the long warm days.

I received a phone call from a judge.

HE had applied for an emergency order in which the children be returned to him immediately.

I calmly explained my points to the judge, also let him know that two weeks had been pre-arranged and that date had yet to pass. A hearing was booked in for a couple of days time, I would attend via telephone.

HIS plea was denied. The children could stay with me.

After much conversation and many hormonal flashes of fury, it was decided that Big girl would go back. She wanted to finish her final year at the school she was already in.

Which was fair enough. Of course every decision I had made was with all of their interests at heart, but I respected her choice.

At the end of August she returned to HIM ready for school in first week of September.

The children with me started their new schools and settled in quite quickly.

There was to be another court hearing as to be expected with that first outcome not being in HIS favour.

Cafcass had to come out and speak with the children, to hear their side and prepare a report for the hearing.

I was to attend via telephone again, I asked my Mum to sit with me.

It was all very reasonable, the report from Cafcass would consider the children's wishes, so without having to be in attendance their voices were heard.

At one point my Mum and I had to stifle laughter as HE took umbrage with something the judge had said and began to shout at and berate the judge.

It was glaringly apparent from this point that we had won.

The three children with me could stay as long as I ensured contact and visits were maintained, a schedule for school holidays was set out. That was that.

After having lost everything seven years before; Here I stood in my new home, safe in the knowledge that I had done my best.

My children were finally where they should be.

With their Mumma.

## Happy Ending

The visits with HIM lasted a while. It was awful for them every single time.

You would have thought being away from HIS children would make HIM more appreciative of their time, perhaps spur HIM on to spend quality time with them creating memories.

This wasn't to be. They were miserable. I would have texts and phone calls telling of boredom, of arguments. Until I promised not to send Baby girl back, ever, each time the kick offs had been that large that Police were called.

I continued to encourage the boys to visit beyond this, it was basically forced at this point. As harsh as that sounds.

I had lived a life having my children kept from me, I didn't want to inflict that on HIM, it wasn't fair. HE however proved that even now they were just pawns in HIS twisted games.


The last time HE saw the boys was the Easter holidays of 2019.

I had been staying with G, which also meant I could spend time with Big girl, who was now attending sixth form college in Newcastle and very content with her blooming adult life and friendship group.

It was a day or two before we were due to head home when I received a phone call to say that Big boy had ran off. I rang him and he told me what had happened, I told him to go back to HIS and that G and I would be round to collect them both.

We actually met Big boy on the way, took him round to HIS. Both boys went about collecting their belongings and getting them into G's truck.

HE stood on HIS doorstep arms crossed over HIS chest and spat some character assassinations of the two boys out before trying to cause a rift between G and I with salacious lies.

We piled in the truck, drove off. There and the I promised them that never did they have to go back there if they didn't wish to. I was done forcing them to have a relationship. That wasn't a relationship.

The family times we have spent here in Wales when G visited or up in Newcastle when we visited, G has spent more quality time with them, been more of a role model and father figure than HE ever had.

Myself and the boys actually had a week in a caravan in Whitley bay in February 2020, visiting G. We had days out, spent time with Big girl and HE was none the wiser.

There have been some dark secrets revealed since I got them away from HIM. I feel immense guilt at not having freed them earlier. But I know that I have done everything that I could. That time and love are great healers. Hopefully having fought the battles that I have, I can impart the wisdom and strength I have acquired to my children. Help them heal the wounds of their childhood and become the very best people that they are destined to be. They are each unique in personality but with shared traumas that will one day just be paragraphs in the stories of their own triumphs.

As a Mumma my role was always to protect them, help them to feel safe and to guide their way. I may have been physically absent for a lot of their formative years, but I never stopped fighting to be there.

I became broken, but slowly, over time, I put each and every one of those shattered pieces back together and came out stronger than anyone would have ever expected.

Each battle gave more strength for the next until eventually, I won the war.

My children and I now walk together into the future ready to face anything life wishes to throw at us.

The year is 2021.

HE no longer has contact with any of the children and they are better for it.

Never give up!

The future is whatever you choose to make it.

I chose to keep being a Mumma.

What will you choose?

# Part Seven

Epilogue

# Epilogue

I wanted to write this book to try and help those of us that have been beaten down by life's experiences.

To potentially send hope, that all is not lost.

That the deep dark pit of despair you languish in is merely a starting point.

There were so many times throughout my journey so far that I felt like giving up.

But I always had the idea that things could get better. That to lay down and die would be giving in to those that wished me harm.

I'm far too stubborn for that.

They don't get to win.

So each and every time I was laying down fractured, seemingly beaten; I pulled myself up, made myself stronger.


There are many books and essays to help everyone to heal.

Each of us are different and what works well for one, may not for another.

But what will help everyone is to sit in your truths.

Know yourself, see your failings, your flaws. Sit with them, accept them.  Then move on. Approach each part of you that needs improving and find a way to improve it.

The answers are there.  Take ownership.

It's not an easy undertaking.  It's ugly.  It's painful.

But, it's also worth it.

I look around at my life today and I am so thankful I am here.

The experiences shared within these pages helped shape me.

I am where I am because I kept fighting.

Because I had faith that if things weren't how I wanted them to be right now, then the story wasn't over.

Happily ever afters don't exist.

But finding happy in more moments each day than the misery that came before.

That exists.